This book is a beautiful reminder that one of the most powerful gifts we can give to our families and to the world is to show up for our own lives and be who we really are.

MEGAN TAMTE, co-CEO and cofounder of EVEREVE

For those who feel defeated, downtrodden, or just plain tired, Melissa Camara Wilkins's gentle, grace-filled encouragement may be exactly what you need to hear.

ANNE BOGEL, author, creator of Modern Mrs. Darcy,
and host of the *What Should I Read Next?* podcast

This is a book for anyone who struggles with feeling like she has to measure up, get it all together, and constantly improve herself. In sharing her story, Melissa reminds us all that you don't have to fix yourself before you're worthy of love and belonging.

ALLISON FALLON, bestselling author and
founder of Find Your Voice

I hadn't even finished the first chapter of *Permission Granted* before I found myself crying tears of relief. Melissa's vulnerable tone is a rare gift in our picture-perfect grammable world, and her stories and subsequent permission slips offer women a simple, audacious possibility to consider: perhaps we already are who we've been frantically trying to become.

JAMIE C. MARTIN, author of *Introverted Mom*
and editor of SimpleHomeschool.net

I didn't know how much I needed *Permission Granted* until I started reading Melissa Camara Wilkins's words. Not only did she give me permission to enter into the messy moments of life and tune myself to the present, but with generous doses of grace and humor alike, she reminded me to love, let myself be love, and let myself receive love. I don't think there's a better gift an author can give a reader.

CARA MEREDITH, author of *The Color of Life:
A Journey Toward Love and Racial Justice*

This book will have you asking yourself hard questions and will give you courage to really listen for the answers. Melissa has written us all a permission slip to discover who we really are, so we can be our whole selves in our real lives.

DANEEN AKERS, author of *Holy Troublemakers*
& Unconventional Saints

Permission Granted

BE WHO YOU WERE MADE TO BE
AND LET GO OF THE REST

Melissa Camara Wilkins

ZONDERVAN®

ZONDERVAN

Permission Granted
Copyright © 2019 by Melissa Camara Wilkins

Requests for information should be addressed to:
Zondervan, *3900 Sparks Dr. SE, Grand Rapids, Michigan 49546*

Zondervan titles may be purchased in bulk for educational, business, fund raising, or promotional use. For information, please email SpecialMarkets@Zondervan.com.

ISBN 978-0-310-35357-7 (softcover)

ISBN 978-0-310-35359-1 (audio)

ISBN 978-0-310-35358-4 (ebook)

Author is represented by The Christopher Ferebee Agency, www.christopherferebee.com.

Interior design: Denise Froelich
Cover design: connie gabbert | design + illustration

Printed in the United States of America

19 20 21 22 23 LSC 10 9 8 7 6 5 4 3 2 1

For Dane,
and for Abigail, Owen, Audrey, Sadie, Eli, and Evelyn.
You are all the best.

Contents

I Am the Worst

Permission to Be Human

Life is complicated. What I've always wanted life to be is . . . simple? Simpler, anyway. I'm not talking about the kind of simplicity that comes from giving away half the furniture and painting the walls white, or sitting around on an empty beach all day, though that doesn't sound so bad. I just mean I've always wanted to feel like I had it all together, like I was qualified to be a person. But no. Life has always been complicated, and most of the time I was pretty sure I was doing it wrong.

In fact, I had a charming personal mantra that went like this: *I am the worst.* It was like an affirmation, except the opposite. Some people say, "I'm good enough, I'm smart enough, and I have what it takes." I said, "Ugh, I should have known."

My phone is out of power? I am the worst at recharging.
Sauce on my shirt? I am the worst at spaghetti.
What was that guy's name? I am the worst at remembering.

Everyone else seemed so confident about existing. *Yes, they seemed to say, I do take up space on this planet and that's cool.*

I, on the other hand, was running late, wearing the wrong shoes, and anxious about whether the twinge in my side meant I was dying of an undiscovered illness, or if I'd just strained a muscle by sneezing while reaching for my sunglasses. In other words, everyone else was pretty much okay and I was kind of a mess, so everyone else was better and I was the worst. This was basically a mathematical law. Or at least logic.

> *Sorry to be slow to reply. I am the worst at email. Or texting. Or commenting on things. Or remembering that we are in the middle of a conversation.*
>
> *Am I in your way? I am the worst at predicting where other people will want to walk and preemptively choosing another place to stand. So sorry. I'll move.*
>
> *I'm sorry we're late. And that I tried to sneak in without being noticed—with all six of my kids. We had a minor emergency involving a hair tie and raspberry jam. I am the worst at getting out the door.*
>
> *And if you've ever in the history of the world left me a voicemail, I will never know because I am the worst at voicemail. I will see the red dot and want to get rid of it, but that is where my skills end. I will never listen to the message, and I will never call you back. I have no idea how to do those things, and I don't even want to learn. I really am the worst at phones.*

If you say it with a half-smile and a shake of your head, it sounds more like a fun status update and less like final judgment.

I said yes when I should have said no? I'm the worst!
I missed something, I overlooked it, I forgot. I'm just the worst.
I don't even want to get out of bed. I'm so tired. I'm the worst.
I can't handle this. I'm not good enough, I'm not strong enough, I
 can't do enough. I am out of everything. I can't breathe. I'm
 the worst.

I was judging myself so other people wouldn't have to, as a helpful little service to us both. I was deciding I came up short before anyone else ever needed to measure. I thought that was my job, because I could see the truth about myself, and the truth was that I had a whole bunch of not-perfect going on inside. I had a whole bunch of not-perfect going on outside, too. The truth looked, to me, like a giant list of things to work on. The least I could do was call it what it was: *the worst*. (You're welcome.)

I did understand all the things that were expected of me. I could see all the Life Rules; I'd just never been able to follow them all—I couldn't follow the rules about looking just right and not being too weird, or the rules about not taking up space (did I mention the six kids?), or the rules about buying all the right things. I've always had way too many feelings to follow the rules about being "low maintenance" or quiet or go-with-the-flow. I couldn't do any of that, but I could at least let you know I understood the program. That was how I made up for not fitting into the system. It was like an existence tax. *The worst.*

Being the worst is exhausting. That's what I was thinking about when I went to hear my friend Jessica speak at her church. I have an on-again, off-again relationship with church. For as long as I can remember, I've understood myself to be a child of God, known and loved. I like Anne Lamott's explanation about God: that we might call God "the animating energy of love we are sometimes bold enough to believe in," or "something unimaginably big, and not us," or goodness, or the divine mystery, or the source of all things, or, as Lamott writes, "for convenience sake, we could just say 'God.'" I've always found God to be a source of comfort, but I haven't always found churches to be quite as welcoming. (And if church is hard for me, as a straight, white, married, middle-class woman, I can't imagine it's a whole lot easier for anyone else.) At its best, church is a beautiful thing—a community of people who gather to remind each other of who they are, to learn and grow together, and to practice being a loving presence in the world. So I kept trying.

Jessica and I weren't *exactly* friends yet, but we'd met a couple of times. I knew her background was in social work. I knew she was going to be talking about brokenness and shame and God and connection. When she said *brokenness*, I understood her to mean *all the things that made me the worst*. Being the worst felt like being broken.

I saw the email invitation and thought, *I'm in*.

I like the idea of working toward my own health and wholeness. Doesn't that sound good? But if you're working on becoming more whole, that means you're walking around aware of your brokenness all the time. You see all the gaps and untidy corners, all the dark places and sticky patches that still need to be worked through. It's complicated. If you're going to make things better, you have to be aware of what needs fixing. And I was very, very aware.

What were you supposed to do if you could see the truth, and you couldn't fix it? What were you supposed to do if you knew you were not perfect, and therefore not okay, and therefore the worst? Maybe Jessica would explain this to me.

I had tried fixing myself, but fixing things hadn't made me better. Fixing things made me tired. Because the truth is, you can't fix everything. Some things just are the way they are. I don't know why.

No matter how many bowls I bought to hold my keys, I never remembered to actually put them there. (I did keep trying though, because the next one I bought might be magic.)

No matter how many times I told myself that my kids had a cold and not the swine flu, I continued to secretly worry that the world was about to end.

No matter how friendly someone might seem, I always suspected that they only let me stay at the party because I brought the sliced fruit.

The truth was that I was messy, and the mess didn't seem to be going anywhere. But if the truth was supposed to set me free, this was not that. I did not feel free. I felt all tied up with my dramatic feelings and my forgetfulness and my disorganization and my never-clean refrigerator shelves.

How did other people hold it all together? How did other people show up everywhere on time and appropriately dressed, with all the required accessories, unruffled and not looking like they lost a battle with hair product on the way in? How did everyone else always know the answers to all the hard questions, like "how are you" and "what's new"? How did they have clean kitchen counters and cars that did not look like a receipt explosion had taken place in the center console? This was what I could not figure out. It's like there was some special thread to sew up your life that I did not have. I was the worst at finding the secret special thread store.

My husband, Dane, and I found seats at Jessica's church, and I tucked my purse-that-was-not-a-diaper-bag-even-if-it-was-full-of-fruit-leathers under my chair. Our kids were not in the room with us, which happened approximately never. I wondered if this could count as a date, even if it was a Sunday morning. Dane squeezed my shoulder. I think that meant yes.

"You are okay—you are good and beautiful—right now," Jessica began, and I thought, *Yes! Yes, you are. All of you people in this room, you are okay. You're good. Some of you are probably amazing! You are loved, you are enough just as you are* . . . and then I realized she thought she meant me, too. That did not sound right.

I peeked at the people in all the other chairs to see if they believed her. I wanted to give her the benefit of the doubt because, between the two of us, she's the one who has a degree in marriage and family therapy. She knows a thing or two about being human, even if she did seem totally wrong about me. This room full of people did not appear to be swimming in the knowledge of their own beauty and worth, either, though. They mostly looked as unsure as I felt.

"And we are *also*," Jessica said, "on a journey toward growth." We are loved right where we are, and we are invited into more wholeness.

Both/and, I wrote down in the little notebook I carry every-where. I like the both/and, because I am all the things: mother and writer, anxious and hopeful, depressed and optimistic, a mess and wearing mascara, hiding and showing up. I was the worst, and I hoped that I wasn't.

Then Jessica started in with all these other unlikely ideas.

"Embracing your worth doesn't require perfection," she said, as though she believed you could be kind of a mess and still be okay. But wasn't the mess how I knew I *wasn't* okay?

She said, "Brokenness does not have to lead to shame," as if she thought your mess might not be your permanent identity. As if you could build something more solid to live out of. As if that feeling of brokenness might be like a burned-out light bulb: it needs attention, but it doesn't mean the whole house needs to be torn down.

"Restoration comes from being known and loved," Jessica went on, "not from shutting out and shutting down." It was almost as if she thought hiding and pretending and trying harder weren't going to fix anything. So weird.

But when you're the worst, you have to shut everyone else out. No one else can understand, because they more or less have it all together and you don't. You know everybody else is doing better than you are. It's in the name: *worst*. That's why you can't trust yourself, either, not for one minute, because if you're the worst, the things you think and feel and want are probably all wrong. You don't have a lot of options. You can hide, you can work harder, you can pretend to be pretty good at being a person, or you can distract yourself, so you don't notice how you compare. Those are the choices. Maybe you can start listening to yourself later, when you've learned to organize a sock drawer or orchestrated world peace. *Come back and we'll talk then*, you tell yourself.

"Judgment has to go," Jessica said, finally. "We have to stop judging ourselves and each other. People are the way they are for a damn good reason."

People are who they are for a damn good reason.

And I am people.

She *did* mean me.

Did she not know that I could never find my other shoe? That I forgot to reply to text messages? That I was constantly disappointing people and getting things wrong and falling short?

"For a damn good reason," Jessica said.

I didn't think I had a good reason, though. I wasn't special; I was just . . . human.

She kept talking, but a tiny glimmer of an idea started stretching itself out in the back of my mind. What if this was just what it meant to be human? What if being a person meant being kind of a mess, even if you tried really hard? What if I wasn't the only one? Everyone else was human, too, as far as I could tell.

I looked around the room again. I've always kept a close eye on everyone else, to see all the places I fall short, so I would know what to work on (or at least what to hide). I looked at all those other people—the ones leaning back in their chairs or nodding along or tucking their hair behind their ears and trying not to make eye contact. Were *they* following all the Life Rules? I looked really, really closely. Most of them had nicer shoes than I had. Most were better than I was at polite conversation, and lots of them were more on time than I was. Three or four looked effortlessly chic and put together. But some weren't following the Pay Attention Rule. Lots weren't following the Appear Obviously Successful at All Times Rule. I couldn't tell how many of them had organized sock drawers.

I glanced at the woman to my right, whom I did not know. What would I say to her, if she turned and told me she was doing everything she could, her absolute best, but she still couldn't get it together? What would I say?

I would tell her the truest thing I know, which is that at her core, her deepest identity is love. She was made in the image of God, and God is love. Love is not what God *does*, love is *who God is*, and love is who she was made to be, too. So the woman sitting next to me—she was made to be love on earth. Love is just what she *is*, the same way that she is blood and bone and muscle. The building blocks of her soul are love. It's what she's made of and what she was made to be.

She is loved, she was made to *be* love in the world, and that will never, ever change.

That's true of everyone. You know this when you hold a tiny baby in your giant arms. That baby is worthy of love. That baby person matters, not because of anything they have done, but because of who they are—and who they are is love wrapped up in flesh. That doesn't become less true as you get older. That's who the woman sitting next to me still was, and is. She is love, and she matters.

That's what I would have told her. I would have reminded her of who she is.

I would have said the same thing to every person in that room.

It was just me who was categorically different. Yes, yes, I was still made of a body and breath held together by love, just like everyone else. That part was the same. But then there was everything else, all the things I was supposed to be and do. I understood the things that were expected of me, and if they were *expected*, that must mean most people—maybe everyone else?— could do them. But I couldn't. So I must not be like everyone else. I must be the worst. This was the understanding I had been working with. It seemed perfectly clear. But here was Jessica, saying otherwise.

"People are," Jessica said again, "the way they are"—she slowed down so we wouldn't miss it—"for a damn good reason."

She did sound convinced.

What was she trying to say? That I didn't have to listen to the voices that told me I had to earn my right to exist, the ones that said I wasn't quite good enough yet but maybe, if I kept trying, someday I'd get there? That I didn't have to keep an ongoing and always-up-to-date list of all my flaws?

Was she really trying to suggest that I wasn't the worst, that I wasn't the burned-out light bulb after all? That I was just human?

Well—yes. That did seem to be her point: that this was what it meant to be human, all the way, completely, messily, understandably human. She did say we were both/and: broken and beloved, imperfect and whole, seen and unseen, held and falling. Maybe that was my good reason.

Maybe that was the only reason.

I'd thought my job was to practice seeing every true thing about myself, but that's not what I had been doing at all. I hadn't been seeing a self, I'd been seeing all my dented pieces and keeping an inventory for insurance purposes. But what if life is just complicated, and me trying to fix it had been making things *more* complicated all along? If I was the way I was for a good reason—well, then, being this way would have to be . . . okay. Being this way would have to be understandable, at least. Where I am would have to be an acceptable place to be, right now.

If Jessica was right—if we are the way we are for a damn good reason, if our *actions* might sometimes be wrong but our *identities* are good, if the worth of our being is not even up for discussion—then maybe we aren't meant to become *better*. Maybe we're meant to become *truer*. What if that's the goal? Not to become something different, but to accept the truth of who you are—the truth that you are a messy, confused, flailing expression of love in the world? Maybe the simplest, truest version of ourselves is that one. Maybe the real work of our lives is to strip away the extra stuff we've added on top, so we can know who we really are. Maybe the work is to stop seeing our true selves as problems to be fixed. Maybe love—the love that animates us, the love that is as close as our breath, the love that is in us and through us, the love that we might call God—keeps offering us invitations to peel back those layers, to see ourselves more clearly, everywhere and all the time.

Trying to fix yourself does not make life less complicated. I know this for sure. I've tried it, and it only makes life more difficult. But what about *being* yourself? Could that make life simpler? Listening to Jessica, I thought it might. And I thought I might give myself permission to try. I would quit making the complicated things more complicated. Maybe that was what I needed all along.

You're not the worst at being human. This is what I had to figure out. You're just human at being human. For a damn good reason.

CHAPTER 2

This Is Why You're
Not Getting Better

Permission to Crack the Shell

Before I was the worst, I'd tried to be the best. Obviously, that didn't work out. My psychiatrist talked me out of it.

I once sat in her office with my baby on my lap. We had already talked about what was going well (the squishy baby, who was charming and happy and growing) and what wasn't (feeling hollowed of all emotions, crying for hours at a time, not sleeping, lurking fears that I might accidentally drop the baby off a balcony even though we lived in a ground floor apartment). Then her pen hovered over her prescription pad.

She spoke like a truth-telling girlfriend, one who has your best interests at heart even if you don't see things in quite the same way. "You know," she said, "you can show up here in your pajamas. I don't care what you wear."

I smiled and nodded as though that was relevant information.

At that moment, my hair was freshly washed and tucked behind a feathered headband. I wore a new shirt, dark-wash jeans, and nude lipstick. I was deeply depressed and dressed as though I were on my way to a lunch date instead of to an appointment with a postpartum specialist. Sure, it had taken everything in me to get ready; I couldn't even drive myself to her office afterward. The thought of having to find a parking space made me want to give up and cancel the appointment. Dane had driven me here and deposited me in the waiting room.

But now, I sat perched on the edge of an easy chair, toes on the ground, waiting for the magic beans (and/or pills) that would make everything right.

They say it takes 10,000 hours of practice to become an expert, and I've been pretending things since I was three years old. I started out pretending to be a ballerina, learned to pretend to be okay with the world as it is, and eventually graduated to pretending to be a moderately competent adult. I pretended not to need anything. I pretended to be well. I pretended I could handle my life. I don't think I'm the only one who's ever done this, either.

I've got everything under control. I can do it all as long as I stop for coffee first. And I'd love to help with that project! Sound familiar?

We're all faking, and we're all experts at it. We pretend to be superheroes instead of practicing being ourselves. No one will ever know, unless we try to fly and fall flat in our shiny unitards. Taking off the reflective tights was my first lesson in simplicity. See, I thought pretending to be perfect was simpler than just being me, but there was a tiny flaw in my plan.

My doctor sighed. "You're working so hard to look like

you're fine," she said, "that you don't have any energy left to actually get better."

It only takes one true sentence to suck all the air out of a room.

I'd had a *plan*. Or if not exactly a plan, at least a sort of nebulous idea about how things worked. I thought that if I looked good, if I tried hard, if I wore the right clothes and smiled at the right times, if I brought a tinkling laugh with me everywhere and left my doubts and whispering fears at home, if I was not needy or whiny or difficult or demanding in any way, then maybe people would like me enough that they would want to see the whole, real me. If they were impressed by the outside part, maybe they wouldn't reject the inside part. I thought I just had to reach a certain standard of perfection to be acceptable, and then once I was accepted, I could let people in on the whole imperfect mess of me. Being perfect was the first step toward being well. This was my genius plan.

So I worked on making things smooth on the outside. *Yes, I will sign up. Yes, I will bring the food. Yes, I will pack the bags, get out the door, say the right thing, do what everyone expects, not upset the system.*

It's a plan that covers over the complication of being human with the complication of pretending not to be.

I told myself—and I really believed it at the time—that if I could just work a little harder at holding everything together, things would be fine. I could stick with the plan. But the body tells its own truth: when you are tired, when you're hungry, when your hormones are out of whack, when you're sick or scared or lonely, a certain irritability comes up, a certain inability to tolerate things that don't usually bother you. The truth is, those things always bothered you; you just hadn't noticed. You were too busy burying that truth, too busy hiding it from yourself. It's only when you're broken and crumbled and cracked down the middle that you have no choice but to notice all those things.

I'd wanted my doctor to help me get back to the plan, and instead, she gave me this: "You're working so hard to look like you're fine that you don't have any energy left to actually get better."

But I needed to get better.

Because at that moment, the thing I was feeling was not sadness.

It felt like emptiness. Not calm. Not peace. Not quiet. Not rest. Just emptiness, like a great gaping void; a hungry, aching nothingness that consumed every feeling, every thought, every bit of light it encountered. The silence roared, so that I did not even notice those things passing me by.

And into that emptiness, whispers would creep, pointing out my abundant flaws. I was not, would never be, a good enough mother for these children. Everything I did, someone else could do better. I could contribute nothing, I could supply nothing, I could provide nothing, I *was* nothing. The nothingness consumed me, as though a black hole had formed where my lungs used to live.

It was the hormones talking, perhaps, the altered brain chemistry. *It will get better, it will get better, it will get better,* I told myself, but I wasn't sure I believed it.

Dane and the children could still bring me tiny, painful stabs of joy—not happiness, not good cheer, but the sharp reminder that somewhere underneath what I felt or didn't feel, all the goodness in my life was still there, connected to me somehow, just out of my reach. It was a piercing awareness of all I was missing. Remembering was good, because it meant that the vacuum had not entirely replaced me. And remembering was terrible, because I could not find my way back.

I tried every natural remedy that might help, as a first line of defense: herbs and supplements, sunshine and movement, medicinal teas, drops and capsules and pellets, but none of them had brought me home to myself.

I knew this was a problem, obviously, but I was kind of hoping no one else would notice, or that it would resolve on its own with enough time—like a lingering cough that interrupts your breathing for weeks, until one day it doesn't anymore. I stuck to the plan, I was just a little . . . flatter. Quieter. Less likely to notice if you spoke to me. What else was I going to do? The way to be okay was to appear to be flawless. I put a sweater on over the black hole and kept going.

My midwives kept checking in on me, even though we were long past our newborn visits. Finally one of them pulled Dane aside. "I need to remind you that depression can be a terminal illness," she said. "Some of these remedies will take months to help. She does not have months."

The midwife found the psychiatrist. Dane made the appointment. I made myself as normal-looking as possible, so as not to disturb the surface of anyone else's reality, and that was how I came to be in her office. I thought she would know what to do to get me back to business as usual.

So when she said, "You're working so hard to look like you're fine that you don't have any energy left to actually get better," I wanted to tell her that she clearly didn't understand. I was actually kind of angry; how did she not see the importance of this cover I had built to hide behind? And then, in the next breath, I knew she was right. I would never be able to make this work. I was feeding my false self and starving my soul. And for what?

So that I could spend my life constructing an admirable shell—one that nothing could get through, one that was pleasing but bland? So that you could smile and wave at it but never be touched by it? So that when I finally dropped under the weight of that shield, people would nod approvingly and say, "Well, she did more or less meet our expectations"? This did not, somehow, seem worth the effort.

A shell feels safe, because nothing gets past it. The only problem is, *nothing gets past it.* You're trying to keep out judgment and fear, but light and love and connection and goodness all bounce right off it, too.

And a black hole—well, a black hole is not nothingness. It's a gravitational field so intense that it has pulled all things into itself. It contains infinite mass, it holds light and darkness together within it. Nothing escapes.

I couldn't feel any of the feelings. I had pulled them all in and shut them all down. Nothing could shine in me just then. But *I* was not nothing, and I was not becoming nothing, and I did not have to hide the truth behind a fancy exterior. There was nothing to hide. I just had to be the thing I was: wild, messy, and freer than I understood.

I don't know if the doctor knew all that, or if she could just see that I had turned brittle around the edges. The smile I had pasted on was drooping on one side. I think the glue holding it up was coming unstuck. I held myself unnaturally, even I could see that. I kept myself at arm's length, like I was something distasteful. Really, I was just afraid of being sucked further into the black hole, but I knew she was right. I couldn't hold my real inside and my fake outside together much longer. They were spinning hard, pulling in opposite directions, and I was going to have to let go.

All the outside stuff—the looking good and keeping up—that stuff would have to die so that my real self—the one I was afraid to let out, the one I thought would drive everyone away, the one I thought wasn't good enough, the one who was needy and hurting and unimpressive—could rise. That tender, frightened, hidden self might not have been better than the self I was showing the world, but it certainly was truer.

But what would happen if I let go—if I quit agreeing to attend my regularly scheduled life, to smile and nod, to tie my hair back and stick to the script, to allow everyone around me to remain oblivious while I sank to a place they could not reach? What if I refused to go quietly anymore? What if I ditched my nice lady costume? What if I showed up in pajamas at the psychiatrist's office? I didn't know where that would lead; I just knew it would be hard and it would hurt, like pulling off a bandage left too long on a wound. Trying to be perfect hurt, too, but it was a dull feeling I'd gotten used to. I knew that pain and what it meant. Letting people in on it felt scarier, like pointing to my own skinned elbows and asking people to poke them. It might be simpler than pretending, but it wouldn't be easier.

I wondered if my doctor would write that all down on a card I could carry around with me everywhere. I would hold it up to show people: *I cannot put on the makeup and stand up straight and tilt my head to the side and smile anymore. I have to choose between that and sanity. Pretty hair loses this round.* It would be my doctor's note, and everybody knows a doctor's note is a valid excuse.

But you do not actually need a doctor's note to choose your own life. You do not need a special pass to be yourself. You can just choose. You just stop chasing after normal and start being real. You stand your ground and say, *I will be all of me. I will show up however I want to. I will wear pajamas all day if I need to. I will tell the truth. I will cry at inopportune moments over things that do not make any sense to anyone else, so that I can also, at other times—eventually— laugh a loud, falling-over kind of laugh until I am gasping for breath. I will make some people uncomfortable, and I will be okay with that. I will close my eyes and take deep breaths. I will take a step back. I will take my time. I will do what I need to do. I will tell the truth some more. I will, I will, I will.*

So I decided to try. I stopped pretending to be fine, and I started using words like *depression* and *anxiety*, *insomnia* and *hard*.

Sometimes, for some people, this goes really well. You tell the truth, and the people around you rise up to tell their truth in solidarity and compassion. Sometimes, for some people, it goes like that.

And then other times, it sucks.

When people asked how I was, and I did not say, "Terrific!" most people nodded and patted my hand, at first. But when healing was slow to find me, and my answers did not change, theirs did.

"What, still?" one woman asked, her nose wrinkled and her lips puckered, as though hearing my words was akin to sucking on a lemon.

"You know, there's no shame in taking meds so you can get back to really *being there* for your family," a friend's husband told me, which did not sound to me like interest in my health and well-being, but what did I know? Another man said the same thing a week later. And another after that. Shame about getting treatment was not actually among my problems—my psychiatrist never even had time to miss me between visits—but men who offered unsolicited opinions might have been.

One faith leader told me he was sorry to hear about my condition, and would be praying for me, while another told me I just didn't have enough joy in my heart—and didn't I know I was supposed to be anxious for nothing? Another suggested that depression meant I was secretly angry with God, which I had no right to be.

"Maybe," I said to Dane, later. "Or I might just have jacked-up neurochemistry."

Sometimes you tell your true story, and the advice is terrible, and the sympathy sounds like misogyny. Sometimes, after a while, everyone else moves on and wishes you would, too.

And sometimes, if the people around you never signed up for all this in the first place—all this difficulty and feeling and reality, this evidence of human frailty—well, they might stop calling, is all. They might stop inviting you in. If you've been building a circle of friends by bobbing around on the surface together, this is where those friends float away.

It would have been easier to stay quiet. It would have been easier to keep wearing concealer and a fake smile.

But simple does not mean easy. Simple means *uncomplicated*. Making things simpler means removing all the complications from inside you, all the layers you've built up to hide who you are and how you feel. Simplicity is when your outside choices and your inside self match up, when your life is telling the truth of your heart. This is not quick-and-easy, surface-level simplicity. This is soul-level simplicity. It's vulnerable, scary work. It's not easy. It did not even magically make me well. Finding your way back to solid ground takes time, and it does not happen all at once. But until I stopped wearing myself out trying to be who I thought I was supposed to be, I didn't have the strength to start getting better.

And yes, when I stopped pretending to be the best, I moved straight into thinking I was the worst. I took off the superhero suit, but I figured if I wasn't super, I wasn't anything. That wasn't true, though. Being the best doesn't work as a way of life. Being the worst doesn't work, either. The only thing that works is being who you are, being who you were made to be. That's who you are behind the shell. It's what remains when you take off the armor.

What you are letting out when you crack open your shell isn't just your own mess. What you are letting out is your truth, and that truth is healing. Truth is nuanced and complicated, but *telling* the truth is simple. You just say what you see and say who you are. Your truth may be made up of fear and anxiety and worry and mistakes and failure, but it is also made of laughter and connection and beauty and wisdom and creativity. (Your truth might also involve prescription medication. Sometimes it helps.) Truth is the beauty and the mess, truth is the falling and the rising, truth is the good stuff and the bad stuff. It's everything that belongs—and everything *does* belong—all mixed up together.

That's where the healing is. It's not in waiting for someone else to give you permission to be human. It's not in hiding the truth when you feel miserable. It's in giving yourself permission to be everything you are—the good things, the hard things, all the things together—on the outside as you are on the inside, with nothing to hide.

CHAPTER 3

Less Busy, More Being

Permission to Stop

I appreciate a good calendar. I used to keep one on the wall in my kitchen, its squares all covered with tidy writing in ballpoint pen.

When Abigail—my oldest daughter—was a toddler, every square was filled in: park days and playdates, outings and appointments, even things like "Call R and A back" and "Library books due!"

Now my calendars are just pretty. If I need to remember something, I set a reminder on my phone and then forget about it. (I am really good at the forgetting part. When those reminders pop up, most of the time I cannot remember what they're talking about. "Take Sadie to L!" Is L a person or a place? Or maybe a time, like "later"? I just hit snooze and hope for the best.)

But when I had only one little person to buckle into a car seat, the squares were all spoken for. Filling up the whole week felt like finishing off a lucky bingo card. *BINGO! BINGO! We have a winner!*

On those filled-up days, I would wake up early, pack a diaper bag with spare clothes, and snacks, and a hat, and sunscreen, and sand toys, then stop at the deli with tiny Abigail to pick up lunch before heading to the playground. Playgroup was at a different park every week, so I had to fight the wave of anxiety that told me I had surely misread the calendar and driven to the wrong place. I was afraid that not only would we be all alone, but we would also have missed out on what everybody else was doing at some other park. When that did not happen (because that never happened), Abigail would climb things and get stuck at the top, and I would try to reach her over my pregnant belly. The adults would attempt to have conversations about peanut butter that were interrupted every forty-two seconds by calls for help up the ladder, requests for apple slices and water bottles, or skinned knees that had to be washed off in drinking fountains. After lunch we would go home for a nap, then back out to the library. We might stop at the grocery store, which felt like possibility in the form of cucumbers and dried lentils. I could imagine making practically anything at the grocery store, even if I was really just going to buy the same pita bread and hummus as always.

Busyness is complicated all on its own. You have to keep one eye on the clock, you have to remember what day it is, you have to know how much time is left before the next thing on your list. But the real question is, why are you keeping yourself so busy? If you can figure that out, you're halfway to making things simpler. (Spoiler alert: It took me a while.)

"What did you two do today?" Dane would ask every night over dinner.

Well, we'd kept in nearly constant motion, at least.

It didn't occur to me that all that running around didn't

actually get me anywhere. I just felt important and special because my days were full of activity.

When someone asked, "How are you?" I did not have to say, "Tired and confused—I don't know if I'm doing the right things with my child and myself and my life. Every decision feels heavy and important and also probably inconsequential in the long-term, and I don't know which feeling to trust. The afternoons are so long—so, so long—and I don't know what to do with them. More laundry? Am I allowed to just read books I want to read and grow tomatoes because I like them, or do I have to be doing something that looks more like work since I'm not earning any dollars at the moment? I don't know if I'm supposed to try to justify that or not. I don't even know if I'm moving in the right direction. How can you tell?"

Instead I could say, "I'm busy! So busy. Always busy. Keeping busy!" Which meant, "I am important, or at least not lazy. My days are not aimless! My life is not meaningless!" That's almost a direct translation.

I was taking the disorientation of new parenthood and turning it in a hundred dizzying directions, so I never had to look right at it. I was distracting myself from all my tiny, gnawing anxieties instead of giving them a voice. I was chasing after feelings of importance instead of asking real questions about purpose and meaning and worth. It wasn't the best plan I ever had, I will say.

And then I had another baby.

A few weeks after Owen was born, I glanced at the calendar. The squares were all scribbled over right up until the day he arrived, and then—nothing. Blank squares as far as the eye could see. (Which, admittedly, was not very far because a month only has thirty days, but that feels like a long time with a newborn.)

If all those things on the calendar had been important, I was losing my grip on what mattered. Or else I had been spending my days on things that had not mattered so much in the first place. Could that be? That could be.

I could feel my sense of direction seeping right out of me. I'd thought I had purpose and I'd thought I had plans, but the whole plan was really just "do the next thing on the next square."

Motion always feels like it matters. And it does, sort of, because movement is a sign of life. Living things are always growing and changing. But busyness is only a shadow of that kind of movement.

Parents are especially susceptible to confusing the two because life with children is full of movement, but not necessarily forward momentum. It's more full of cyclical rhythms that are forever coming undone. You put your child to bed, and she wakes up in the morning and needs to be put to bed again the next day. You wash all the clothes and put them away, but they're dirty again five minutes later, and all the progress you thought you'd made has disappeared. You make breakfast, you make snacks, you make lunch, you make snacks, you make dinner and also snacks. Then you make breakfast again. You tell your toddler to play on the floor instead of climbing the walls, he seems to understand, and then before you have time to sneeze, he is standing on tiptoe trying to reach the light fixture that hangs over the kitchen table. There is always movement, but it's running in circles and jumping on the furniture.

And what are the markers of success for a parent? You move in the same direction until you cross the finish line? There is no finish line. Are you getting closer to your goal? Your goal is to help that child who is currently putting spaghetti in her hair to one day become a fully functioning adult member of society. Are we closer today than yesterday, when she ate Play-Doh?

What are the markers of success for *anyone*? You have an enduring sense of wholeness, you make meaningful and lasting contributions to the world at large, you make space for other people to step into their own purpose and worth? These are not the kinds of things a person can accomplish by next Thursday.

Busy at least looks like you're working hard at the process.

Process is a marvelous place to focus, but I could have chosen to build my process on some criteria other than "moving all our legs faster than a beetle flipped on its back." Maybe I could have asked myself whether I was enjoying the process of my life, or whether we were strengthening and deepening our relationships, or whether I was showing up as myself in my days. That would have been another way to think about process. Not how much I did, not how fast I moved, not did I get anywhere today, but how present was I, and how aware. Those could have been simpler markers of being on the right track.

I did not think of those, though. I was too intent on jumping the checkers around the board at all times. I didn't care where they were going, only that they kept moving. It's interesting, it's a way to play—it's just that it is, at the end of the day, pointless. Busy feels important, but it isn't building anything lasting.

I hadn't noticed. I had let my identity and my worth get all tied up in the busyness until it looked to me like a badge of honor.

Someone would say, "Let's try to get together sometime," and I wouldn't say yes, and I wouldn't say no—such boring, straightforward answers. There's no intrigue in a yes or a no.

Instead I could say, "Let's do that! I'll have to check my calendar." It's like following that old dating advice about not being too available; If I'm busy, I must be in demand. What I might be busy doing, well, that is mysterious and interesting. Just the fact that I'm busy suggests that other people want me around. It says that I must be worth knowing, doesn't it?

But keeping busy creates days that are full, not days that are fulfilling. That's not a journey, that's a carousel.

When I stood in front of that calendar with Owen in my arms and Abigail hanging on my knees, I realized: I hadn't been filling my days with meaning; I'd just been passing the time.

I had to be still before I could even notice. I had to stop flitting from place to place like a crazed hummingbird. I hadn't left myself any space for stillness, and what you find when you hold still is . . . *you*.

Whatever feelings you discover in that stillness, whatever desires, whatever hopes, whatever frustrations, whatever disappointments, whatever delights, whatever surprising joys, whatever fierce longings and deep resentments, whatever loves and attachments, they are yours, they are there for a good reason, and they have been humming along under the surface, just waiting for you to notice.

I didn't know that making myself unavailable as a state of being made me unavailable to myself, too. I hadn't been available to listen for what I wanted and what I didn't. I hadn't been available to hear the whisperings of my own soul. I hadn't had time to wonder who I was, or who I was becoming, or if I liked this person. If you're unavailable to yourself, you never have to notice what you aren't asking.

I wasn't asking the hard questions—the ones I didn't know the answers to, the ones that had no answers, the ones that had answers I wasn't sure I'd like.

Who am I now? Am I okay? Am I supposed to know what I'm doing?

I didn't want to look at the answers to those questions, so I found something else to look at instead, something that would make me forget how unsettled I felt. There are plenty of options when you don't want to look at your life. I can sit on my couch and pull out my phone, and let it tell me what's going on in the world instead of wondering what's going on in my heart. I can post a photo to Instagram and wait for the little hearts to pop up, to tell me that other people like the shiny, filtered version of my life instead of asking how I feel about the real thing.

This is why we keep our personal distraction devices safely tucked in our pockets all day long. We're choosing to be available to something, just not to ourselves.

I had been looking to my calendar for evidence that someone, somewhere wanted me at all times. That little bit of reassurance could quiet the questions until the next distraction arrived.

Was I the best? Was I the worst? Who could say, really?

I'd thought that pinging between activities was the same thing as knowing other people and being known by them. I saw people every day! I saw the same people every week! But I had always bounced on to the next conversation before the last one was even finished. Busy doesn't leave room for connection, only for collection. You collect people, and activities, and moments, and conversations, and you cross them off your list.

I thought busyness meant intimacy, but it only meant proximity. I thought slowing down would make me a hermit. I thought my choices might be between trivial conversation or no conversation, but that wasn't true. Busyness is a weedy garden; it's too many seedlings all planted in one pot, so nothing can thrive. There's no room for roots. Planting a lot feels purposeful, but plant too much and nothing will grow.

Standing in my kitchen, keeping us all afloat between sleeps,

I could not plant one more thing. All I could do was be who I was, where I was.

I had been afraid of the empty canvas that was my life, too anxious to face the blank pages that were my days. I thought I had to fill them up, as fast and as full as I could manage. Busyness was such a good place to hide, I wouldn't have given it up if it hadn't slipped right out of my fingers. Without busyness, how would anyone know I was important? How would anyone know I mattered? How would I know?

Apparently, I was going to find out.

Because when I looked away from the calendar, I discovered that I wasn't sure I wanted to fill it back up. This raised the question of what I *did* want instead.

The calendar did not seem to know the answer to that.

Back in the kitchen, I walked away from the calendar, because it was empty and had nothing to tell me.

Then I walked back to look again.

Still empty. Nothing to see. No new markers of my worth, no more than had been there five minutes ago.

This was not helping me avoid my questions.

Even as I changed diapers and read stories and baked potatoes and took showers and trimmed tiny nails, the questions remained. *Who am I now? Am I okay?*

And as I held those questions, as I waited with them and did not try to cover over them or explain them away, the weirdest thing happened. A quiet, sure voice inside me rose up to answer them.

Who am I now? *Still me, just attached to more people—the way a starfish is attached to its arms.*

Really? *It's a me with more depth, with a wider perspective, with shifted priorities. But yes, still me.*

Do I still matter? *The same amount as before. My worth couldn't have come from something that can be changed with a phone call and a ballpoint pen.*

Even my body was waiting to give me answers when I was ready to listen. I gave myself permission to pay attention to what filled me up and what drained me. I gave myself permission to notice what gave me life, and what felt like a chore. It wasn't hard to tell the difference, once I started paying attention.

I hadn't known that making yourself available to the questions makes you available to the answers, too.

The answers were always there. Those blank calendar squares were not empty; they were *open*, and openness meant possibility.

Avoiding the questions because of what the answers *might be* is so much more complicated than just finding out what the answers *are*. When you finally look right at your real life to see who you are, and where you are, and what you feel—even if you don't like what you find—at least you know. And once you know, you can start to do something about it.

It's simpler to make your life a place you want to be than to spend your days running away from it. Being a person is complicated enough without living a life you don't believe in.

Now I know: my calendar is not a tool to measure my worth. My calendar is a Band-Aid for my ridiculous memory and a place to find out what day it is because I have no idea, and that is all. I don't need outside validation, because I am not meant to be a parking ticket; I am meant to be love in the world.

Now I know. It wasn't until busyness slipped out of my hands that I began to realize: when I quit being busy, I could finally just *be*.

CHAPTER 4

About That Fire

Permission to Belong to Yourself

It's funny, what we are willing to do in order to feel like we belong to something. It hardly even matters what that something is: a group of friends, a bunch of coworkers, a school, a church, a family.

We'll wear different clothes, pretend to be a morning person, sing along to music we would never have chosen on our own, try to convince ourselves we actually do like that new fusion restaurant around the corner. We say things like, "Oh, she didn't mean it like *that*," and "Someday he'll understand," and "I can wait." We let ourselves believe that if we want to belong, all we have to do is change little things about ourselves—we just have to become a little bit different, or better, or the kind of person who pays closer attention and can remember where all the land mines are.

When all else fails, I tell people they have pretty shoes. It's usually true, and no one ever kicks you out of their circle for noticing their shoes.

As I slowed down, as I stopped being busy and practiced telling the truth about who I was and what I needed, I started to notice something. I noticed that my community was made up of people who all *agreed*. That was the common bond: thinking the same things and having the same answers to the same questions. We didn't gather together around a common purpose, or a common history, or a shared family, or a shared neighborhood, or a PTA board. We didn't belong to a culture where community was part of the fabric of our daily lives, where our interactions might be governed by bonds of love and tradition developed over generations. That wasn't why we gathered. We gathered because we had the same answers to a handful of questions that seemed really important. Everyone agreed that these were the right answers, and that agreement bound us together.

The only problem was, I didn't actually agree.

I mean, I agreed with some of it. The questions that were biggest and broadest and widest? We would have answered those similarly. We would have agreed that God is love, and that God is truth. We would have agreed that there is something compelling about learning to walk in the ways of love. But on everything else—the questions about who was in and who was out, and whose voices mattered, and who we were meant to be, and what love looked like—to all of those other questions, we had different answers.

But belonging worked by matching up our outsides—by having the same answers and by agreeing on how important those answers were—instead of by recognizing that we're all the same underneath. The outside isn't all there is. But belonging worked by matching up our outsides—by having the same answers and by agreeing on how important those answers were—instead of by recognizing that we're all the same underneath. The outside isn't all there is. You do have a self apart from everyone else's expectations. There is a self that came before you learned about the Life Rules, before you learned about fitting in and playing nice. Your true self is the core of your being, and it does not need to be told who to be or how to be.

I picked up Richard Rohr's book *Immortal Diamond*, about the search for the true self, and read that underneath everything else, the true self is "where matter and spirit finally operate as one, where divine and human are held in one container."[1] Some might say your true self is who you are in God—in the God that is love, the God that is truth. Another way to say it, then, is this: *Your true self is who you are in love. Your true self is who you are in truth.* This is who you are apart from all the labels and identities you've collected. You are not your job, not your neighborhood, not your relationships, not your awards or your embarrassments, not even your history, though of course all those things shape how you walk through the world. Your true self is deeper than all of that. Your true self is the calm at the center of your storm. Your true self is love. It's the presence of love right here and right now, in you.

Richard Rohr even says that "once your soul comes to your true self, it can amazingly let go and be almost anything except selfish or separate."[2]

Your true self, in other words, can't be a jerk. It doesn't believe in its own separateness, so your true self hurts when others are hurt and celebrates other people's freedom like it's your own.

But we weren't connecting as our true selves. We weren't even acting as though everyone had something beautiful to offer. We weren't recognizing that we're all meant to be different, all meant to be ourselves, and that our differences—even differences of opinion—can make us stronger. Living with those differences opens up our world, widening our perspective and growing our compassion and expanding our understanding of belonging. Instead, we were pulling out one narrow slice of our social selves—the selves we show to the world—and comparing those. If the little slice that held your answers to a handful of specific questions matched, then you belonged.

And I wanted to belong. I wanted to belong so much, because I had absorbed the idea that community was a requirement and a responsibility, and because I *did* agree with some of the things, and because belonging is one of those basic human needs that we all have.

I tried to belong as my mismatched self. I would speak up, and disagree, and then watch as the faces of the people around me closed right off. I paid attention as every discussion had to come back around to those shared answers, the ones that could only be questioned if the question was followed up with the right answer.

The people in those communities were mostly lovely and dear and doing their best to live into the system they were devoted to. Maybe that system brought them life, even as it was draining me. But it *was* draining me, and for a while it seemed that everything I said ended with someone pressing their lips together hard and folding their arms across their chest. I could understand why. When communities are built around everyone thinking the same things, disagreement is not welcome. Disagreement is, in fact, risky. It threatens to shake the whole foundation, and it has to be contained.

I just didn't want to be contained.

So when my questions were not met with interest, when voicing my disagreement led to debate instead of discussion, containment instead of curiosity—I got quiet. I stopped saying anything of consequence at all, and my voice withered.

I started telling people they had pretty shoes.

This was a good thing to say when I had to speak. I was looking down more often than not, so it was something I noticed.

I would be in conversations where the other person would talk, and the thing I wanted to say—the thing that made sense to me—sounded like:

"No. No, I cannot do that. No, I do not agree. No, I do not think that is a good idea."

Or, "Not everyone is welcome here. I think everyone should be welcome here. Maybe with the small exception of, say, the Stay Puft Marshmallow Man from *Ghostbusters*. But everyone else."

Or, "We seem afraid to listen. Why are we afraid to listen?"

Or, "Why are we building walls instead of building bridges? Why are we building a smaller box instead of a bigger table?"

But I was pretty sure that was not how the conversation was supposed to go, so instead I said nothing. I added a layer of silence between who I was and what the world could see, and with that armor in place, I could hold on to the labels I wanted—labels like "friend" and "included" and "liked." I could see how those labels were bound up in expectations about opinions and behavior and rules and judgment—but I couldn't see how to untangle the ones that fit from the rest.

So I would say: "I like your shoes!"

And then later I would say to Dane or to my sister, "This thing happened, and what I *really* wanted to say was . . ." (Dane and my sister are already stuck with me, so I can say all the things to them.) I was glad to let the words out but complaining quietly in my own living room didn't feel expansive or open or loving to anyone, not even to my own self.

I started to dread being with other people, because being present and invisible hurts. We all want to be seen and known, not just take up space. It's like that need was written right across our hearts, and when we hide ourselves, we're turning off the oxygen in the room.

Grumbling, dreading, seething politely: these do not do much to bring people together. Showing up silent and invisible doesn't do it, either.

And the voice inside me, the one I could hear when I got still and quiet and listened, that voice was not having it.

"This is not me," the voice whispered. "This keeping quiet, this not-using-my-voice, this saying the right thing (which is really the wrong thing), this is not me. This does not feel right." Keeping quiet felt like wearing a cheap shirt with a scratchy tag. You can keep rubbing at that itch until your skin is raw, but it's never going to go away until you *change your freaking shirt.*

Scrolling Facebook one day—as you do when you have no one to talk to out loud—I read this from Elizabeth Gilbert:

> "Most of us, at some point in our lives (unless we have done everything perfectly . . . which is: nobody) will have to face a terrible moment in which we realize that we have somehow ended up in the wrong place—or, at least, in a very bad place."

When that realization comes, we may not know what to do next, she says. But what we do know is, "not this."[3]

I could hear the "not this" inside me, I just couldn't tell what it was saying no *to*, exactly. I wanted to belong, and I wanted to be myself, but being myself was making me *not* belong. Something was not working here. "Not this," the voice inside me whispered.

"What if we stop?" Dane asked, because it was his community, too. "What if we just quit everything for now?" We could leave if we wanted to. All that held us together was agreeing, after all.

"But where will we go? What will we do instead?" I wanted to know, because the point of seething in silence was at least to get some belonging out of the deal. If I was going to walk away, I wanted to be moving in a purposeful direction, toward some other sense of community and belonging and life.

"Nowhere," he said. "What if we do nothing—we don't try anything new, we don't go anywhere else, we don't look for new community, we don't even *talk* about it for a while?"

There was A Look on my face; I know there was. He wanted to just give up everything I had been trying to hold on to? Yes, I had been trying to hold onto it the way you might try to keep an angry lizard in your pocket. (I never said the holding on was a good idea.) But—just let go and be without it? And not even run around in a frenzy, trying to replace what I thought I had lost? Just . . . do *nothing*?

I had no other ideas, though, and who wants to try to force a lizard into their pocket anyway? Some people don't. Some people let the lizard be a lizard, and they don't try to convince it to be something else.

"Not this," said my inner voice, again and again and again. Some of us are out of practice at listening for that voice, and some of us never learned how. Some of us were taught not to trust our own inner voices—we were told to listen to an outside voice and obey. That idea is convenient—it doesn't require a lot of free will or decision-making, and the status quo rarely gets upended—but you do not need an outside authority to tell you who you are and why you're here. You came equipped with those truths inside you.

Your inner voice is the voice that comes from your true self. It rises up from connection, from truth, from love, from goodness, from the intersection of matter and spirit, of human and the divine. Your true voice is not the tapes that run in your head. Your true voice does not think you're the worst. Your true voice is not the voice of your culture, or your mother, or your elementary school principal. Call it what you want: the still, small voice inside, the voice of the divine, your conscience, your intuition, your inner knowing, the nudging of the Spirit. It is the voice that rises up within you when you quiet all the other noises.

It does not tell you to take what you want, or to feed your comfort and idolize your own security. It does not tell you to look the other way and ignore everyone else's needs—and it does not tell you to ignore your own, either. It does not tell you to run from the pain that comes along with being human. Your inner voice comes from your true self, the self that you are, in love and in truth. That's why your inner voice is trustworthy—because it comes from that place of truth and love.

I was just afraid that what I was hearing—the "not this" that kept bubbling up inside me—was the equivalent of telling me to give up on sunshine and fresh air and leafy greens. Was my inner voice basically telling me to hole up with a carton of ice cream in my very own cave? I didn't know. I tried asking myself, *Why not this?* And I listened. I wanted to know, did the answers sound like me, like my best, most secure self talking? Did the reasons I was hearing sound like truth and like love?

Your truest voice sounds like compassion for yourself and for the people around you. It sounds like love for who you really are. It whispers acceptance over your past and quiet confidence into your present. It feels like a nudge in the right direction. It feels like you.

And still, sometimes you'll get it wrong. Sometimes you'll think you're listening, and later you realize you weren't really paying attention at all. Sometimes you'll make the best choice you can, and later you learn differently. Okay. You don't have to be right all the time. (You won't be right all the time.) But in the meantime, doing your best to listen well and practicing trusting yourself are not bad things to do.

So I might have been wrong, but that inner knowing, that persistent nudging, was telling me, "Not this," and the reasons why sounded like, "because this is not bringing you life." Because institutions—even institutions that call themselves communities—are supposed to sustain people, not just be sustained by people.

That *did* sound like truth and love.

Which is great and all, but what was going to *actually happen* if I stepped off the path of existing community, stepped out of the conversation where I knew the scripted lines, stepped away from the labels that marked me as included? What would happen in that wilderness?

Brené Brown says that the wilderness is where true connection is born. "When we are willing to risk venturing into the wilderness, and even becoming our own wilderness, we feel the deepest connection to our true self and to what matters most,"[4] she writes, and it seemed to me that if I was going to figure out which direction to walk in, I was going to have to find that connection first.

Speaking up, being myself—these things had not brought me community. But *not* being true to myself hadn't brought me what I wanted, either. If I couldn't control that part—if I couldn't control anyone else's reactions or choices or whether they wanted me around—what was I supposed to do? Showing up as myself would at least bring me back into harmony, lining up who I was on the inside and how I was on the outside all over again.

So I stopped. I stopped arguing and I stopped not arguing. I walked away from every community we'd tried to fit into. I declined invitations. I didn't get up early in the mornings for meetups or gatherings or events. I found myself suddenly, again, with whole swaths of space in my life. There was the now-familiar space on my calendar, but there was also space in my mind once I stopped composing silent arguments in my head all the time. It felt, at first, like a stripping away. It felt like grief, but the grief wasn't for the loss of rhythm and routine or even of relationships—it was grief for what never was. The space I'd opened up had never been filled with belonging; it had been filled with trying to earn belonging.

I could have filled it right back up again, all that empty space. But instead I just . . . didn't. I thought that since I'd never tried it before, I'd see what Dane's plan of *do nothing* looked like. I slept in, I read more, and I stayed home, or I took my kids out or I went places I felt like going. I didn't follow anyone else's calendar. I didn't try to explain myself to anyone else. I didn't even feel guilty about that.

I sat on my couch and had space to listen—not to my inner

voice arguing with other people, but to my inner voice rising up to point out what I needed.

Because the truth is, you know what you need. When you quiet the outside voices telling you what you should do and how you should be—even if the outside voices all have really good ideas—and ask yourself what you want, what you need, what you prefer, what you choose: you know. All the things I had been taught about the importance of community—that without it, you would grow cold like a piece of coal removed from the fire of belonging—was not the whole story. The whole story was that the fire could sustain you, or the fire could burn you, and if you want to find life around that fire, you have to be able to bring your whole self into the light. Before I moved toward the fire—any fire—again, I needed to let my burns heal.

So I lived for a while without the distracting dance of those flames, and eventually, instead of thinking about the empty fire-pit, I got comfortable with what I had, which was openness and the ability to feel like myself everywhere in my life.

There in the wilderness, I found that I did not need the labels and masks and costumes that did not fit after all. It was no loss to leave them behind, because they were just outside pieces. They did not change who I was inside.

It would be okay to disagree with a whole group of people and still be in some kind of relationship with them. It would be okay to be cast out of their circle, too. It would be okay to be misunderstood. Whatever happened on the outside would be okay, because on the inside, I was learning to listen to myself and to trust what I heard. I was learning to belong to myself.

On the other side of that grief was a lightness, a lifting of expectations that I should never have let fall across my shoulders.

I still didn't know what would happen when I brought my whole self into new spaces. When I disagreed out loud, when I didn't mention their shoes at all—would anyone understand, or would everyone take three steps back every time I opened my mouth and all the wrong words started falling out?

I didn't know, but I knew I could not continue to carve away pieces of myself in order to fit in. Belonging is not about agreeing or disagreeing; it's about allowing myself to show up no matter what happens and trusting that if I want to belong to anything else, first I have to belong to myself. So I decided to go with the simplest plan. The simplest plan was to say all the things and not pretend that my outside layers—my opinions, my beliefs, my position, my acceptance, my labels, my costumes—were anything different than what they are, just like I had stopped pretending my inside self was anything different than what it is.

It was possible that if I was my real self, no one would like me. It was possible that no one would ever invite me to belong to their club. Maybe no one would want to be my friend, and everyone would turn and talk to someone else when they saw me coming toward the snack table.

It's easier not to deal with all that. It's easier to buy a new outfit to wear, and smile when you don't mean it, and say "Fine, fine, I'm fine, how are you?" when anyone gets close enough to ask. But "easier" is not quite the same as "leads to a sense of integrity and emotional health and spiritual growth and personal fulfillment." They don't even sound similar, not really.

Anyway, I already had no community to belong to, and I had learned to be comfortable with that. I had learned to be comfortable with myself. I had nothing to lose.

So I tried saying all the awkward things out loud.

"What did you mean by that?"

"I don't agree."

"Why do you think so?"

"I could be wrong, but I'm going to try this anyway."

"That's not for me."

"Why does that seem important to you?"

"I can't."

And I was right; not everyone was excited about this. That is the trade-off. People can see me, and they might not like me. But I will like me, and I will trust me, and I will show up. I will belong to myself, and that is already enough.

CHAPTER 5

Patience, Kindness, and Vitamin D

Permission to Change the Equation

As a parent, I think helping kids develop independence and confidence is important. I also think not letting kids get eaten by wolves is important. It's hard to tell which one to prioritize in any given situation. Parenting is complicated like that.

When my daughter Audrey was nine and my daughter Sadie was seven, they went through a serious we-want-to-go-camping phase. They had never been camping, they didn't really know what camping involved, and I'm pretty sure they would have hiked all the way back home again on foot once they saw what campground bathrooms were like. But someone had given Audrey a four-person pop-up tent for her birthday, and she and Sadie wanted to pitch it in the backyard so they could live in it, maybe forever? They were willing to sleep there all summer, at least.

This was exactly what I wanted for them. Growing their self-confidence! Learning what they could do! Being independent and responsible for themselves! Pitching a tent! Being uncomfortable and learning they could handle it. Possible mosquito bites. (I did not actually want that part.) Good, clean dirt. Flashlights and shadow puppets. *Yes,* I wanted to say, *go for it! You'll be tired and cranky the next day, but I will not have had to drive to a campsite and there will be no extra laundry. Let's do this thing.*

The only problem with this plan was, we didn't actually have a backyard. We had a patio with a half-wall. We could see our neighbors' heads as they walked their dogs up and down the hill. The street on the other side was a great place to park if you didn't have a driveway in our neighborhood, and people came and went at all hours. Conveniently, that street connected right over to a wider, faster-moving road that would take you out of our residential neighborhood and off to anywhere. So while I wasn't worried about bears knocking down the tent, I couldn't shake the idea that someone might hop into the yard, snatch them up, and be halfway to Arizona before we even noticed. I've been to Arizona. It's a nice place, but still.

Even apart from the Arizona factor, there was the nature factor. On the other side of our house—away from where strangers parked—was a little nature preserve with water running through it. (There wasn't enough water to call it a creek, but enough that you could safely call it a moving puddle.) Bunnies lived in there and hopped into our yard every night to eat our one little patch of grass and anything else we planted. Coyotes also lived in there (because: bunnies). We would hear the coyotes howling in the evening, and sometimes late into the night. Once, while we were sitting outside, a coyote poked its head through the fence surrounding the not-a-creek and looked at us. "Hello," it seemed to say. "Anyone available for dinner?" We backed into the house and shut the door.

So when Audrey and Sadie asked to sleep out in the tent, all of this whooshed through my mind. *People-cars-no-privacy-hungry-coyotes-good-mom-bad-mom-camping-fun-danger-coyotes-also-people.* The fear siren in my head started blaring: *Not this! Not this! Not this!*

Of course you can sleep out there! I wanted to say.

"It's kind of sketchy!" I said instead.

I thought the rule was supposed to be that I face my fears and get over them. That is the memo I got. My kids deserve the best version of me, don't they? They deserve the version that isn't stuck or small. They deserve the version that's free, the one that has no fears or limitations. The version that looks like everyone else.

And anyway, I want to chase curiosity, not fear. I wanted to be curious about what my kids would learn by fake-camping. How would they grow? Would they have more self-awareness, a better understanding of who they are and what they are capable of? Think of all they could accomplish in life if I would just let them sleep in a tent crammed in between a half-wall and our back door!

I was curious about the fear, too. Why was I so afraid? Fear might be off base, but it is trying to protect you. It's just that sometimes, it's trying to protect us by ensuring our survival, and other times it's trying to protect us by keeping us inside a familiar little bubble. If you follow *that* fear, you'll never try things like sriracha or frozen hot chocolate, and you'll have significantly fewer interesting friends. Listening, learning, loving, growing—these are all bubble-bursting endeavors.

So was this tent fear one of those bubble fears? Was I right to worry? Was I wrong? How much weight should I give to developing independence, and how much should I give to the possibility of disaster? This was a complicated equation, and I could not make it balance.

Likelihood that this experience would grow their confidence: 40 percent.

Likelihood that they would wake up unchanged except for being cranky because of sleeping on the cold deck: 60 percent.

Likelihood of being eaten by coyotes or relocated to another state: low.

Likelihood that I would stay awake all night just in case: 100 percent.

I do not even know what to do with that math.

What if I choose wrong? How do I choose camping?

———

When my friend Megan came over with her kids the next day, the tent was still set up on the patio. "Are you guys going camping?" she asked, reasonably.

"Well!" I took a deep breath. "Not exactly." I told her how I had let the girls fall asleep out there, but then couldn't sleep myself. My body just stayed on high alert, listening for potential backyard danger and leaping out of bed every time a car door opened or shut anywhere along the street. At three a.m., Dane had suggested we bring Audrey and Sadie inside, and we'd relocated their sleeping bags to the couch.

"It's indoor camping!" I had whispered.

"No," they whispered back.

Maybe I was supposed to do the things I was afraid of, but actually trying to do them was making me break out in hives.

Megan did not laugh or tell me to take a sleeping pill. Instead, she looked out in the yard, then at me. She nodded. She poured a tall glass of water in my kitchen. "You don't want to be driven by fear," she said, "but you need to honor your own comfort level, too."

My own comfort level. This was not something I had thought I could factor in. My feelings weren't as valid as my kids' need to sleep in a tent, were they? That didn't seem like legit decision-making criteria.

"Anyway, we were raised on Stranger Danger," Megan said. "It's not our fault we see everything as a disaster waiting to happen. That's what they taught us."

She had a point. The idea that unguarded children are always one lost puppy away from doom was basically the defining theme of a 1980s childhood. (Well, that along with dubious cartoon entertainment and neon pants.) Fear of tents was baked into me from the beginning.

———

Later I went to see Sheena, my friend who is also my chiropractor, and who lets me talk at her as though she is my therapist. "How are you?" she asked, and she mostly meant things like, do you have any pinched nerves or sore muscles?

"I am really anxious!" I said. "Super anxious. Audrey and Sadie want to sleep in a tent."

She made my spine pop sixteen different ways.

We talked for a few minutes, about me not being God and therefore not being in control of the universe. But that was my problem. I already knew I wasn't in control. I couldn't control the coyotes that might be looking for a snack in a backyard-tent-shaped wrapper. I couldn't control the traffic patterns of the neighborhood. I couldn't control whether a tent turned out to be a growth experience or a form of sleep deprivation. (For the kids. I already knew it was a form of sleep deprivation for me.) How was I supposed to keep everybody safe and happy when I couldn't control anything?

"Well," Sheena said, "in the meantime, how about self-care? Extra sleep, good soup, fresh air? Maybe move your body?"

Was that really an approved plan? Listening to your body instead of doing the thing you thought you were supposed to do? That sounded like a cop-out. I could imagine all the other parents of suburban children pitching tents in the yard, then waving goodnight from their sliding glass doors. Those other imaginary parents did not have a hard time with this, so I shouldn't, either. When I thought about it, I did not know any parents whose kids slept in tents in the backyard, but they were probably out there somewhere, being better than me and raising kids to have super tent powers. Meanwhile, I was keeping my kids from developing their coyote defense skills.

Having kids who sleep indoors all night sounded like staying small in my shell instead of forcing myself to grow and change no matter how painful that turned out to be. It sounded like leaving the sticky bandage on forever instead of ripping it off. Yes, ripping it off would take all the hair and some of the skin with it. No pain, no gain?

But there's more than one way to remove a bandage. The options aren't actually *stay the same* versus *be in pain*. Are they?

"Can we sleep in the tent again tonight?" Sadie asked.

"But *all night* this time?" Audrey clarified, because she was having none of this be-relocated-when-mom-decides-she-finally-has-to-sleep business.

The fearless version of me would say yes. *Yes, go ahead.* Unfortunately, I have never met that version of me. I do not think she exists. There's only this version, the one that is sometimes afraid. The one that—if she says yes at all—says yes when she means no, kicking open a gap between who she is inside and who she is pretending to be on the outside. That is not freedom; that is stupid. I am the way I am for a damn good reason. Yes, we can debate whether the 1980s count as a "good" reason. Yes, we all need healing. Yes, I will keep growing. But the way I am today is not wrong; it just *is*. I can't show up as anyone else, not even as an Ideal Mother Who Has No Fears. Being okay with yourself *as you are right now* is simpler than trying to force yourself to be who you think you're supposed to be. Maybe that other way of being, the one I can imagine, the one I think is better—maybe that way is good, and maybe I'll get there. But that's not where I am right now.

And yet there were Audrey and Sadie, with their hopeful eyes and their original song titled, "Please, Mom?" They were singing it in rounds.

But how were they supposed to grow up to be women who stand in their truth if they were watching me hide from mine?

I decided to try something different. I did not ask myself what I was supposed to think and feel. I only asked what I actually did feel. My gut did not say, "Get over it." My gut said, "COYOTES." Walking through pain is one way to grow, but telling the truth is another. And the truth was that I was ignoring my own gut because I didn't want to disappoint my girls.

I took a deep breath and told the truth. "No," I said. "No, you cannot stay in the tent all night. You can fall asleep out there if you want to, and I will bring you back inside before I go to bed. You can sleep in your sleeping bags in the house with the doors locked."

This, they decided, was a terrible plan. No fun at all. Horrible. No one could survive this plan; it was so bad and so boring. There was no point to even owning sleeping bags if you couldn't sleep with the coyotes!

I listened to all this. I nodded and sympathized and nodded some more, and I did not change my answer. I stirred the vegetable soup and I penciled in an early bedtime. "No," I said again. "You cannot sleep outside, because if you sleep outside, I cannot sleep inside. But look, you can do other things. You can fall asleep outside. You can camp in the backyard all day long. You can pitch the tent and take down the tent and pitch it again. You can choose a nature trail, and I will take you for a hike. You can take a walk in the rain the next time it rains. You can go to the library all by yourself sometimes, because there are no coyotes there. You can rake the leaves when they fall, and you can jump in them, which has nothing to do with building your independence but does involve a lot of mud."

They looked at me like I did not understand the meaning of tents.

"But that is not sleeping in the tent," they said.

"I know," I said. "But it's what we can do."

That's my boundary. I have to be able to sleep, so they have to sleep inside. I'm not developmentally ready yet for anyone to sleep outside. I may be a late-blooming parent, just like some toddlers are late walkers. You don't try to force a baby to walk before they're ready. Pushing just makes everyone miserable.

Once camping was off the table, I had room to breathe. I didn't have to consider and reconsider and second-guess myself and tell myself all the things that were terrible about my decision.

I walked out to the front yard, put my bare feet in the dirt, and felt the late afternoon sun on my face. A prescription of patience with where I am, kindness for myself, and vitamin D is not such a bad starting place, I decided.

My kids might have been better off with the carefree, camping-happy parents in my head, the ones who always make the right decisions, the ones who never worry and never get bored and never have work to do, but they did not get those parents. They got me, and they got Dane (who does not have strong feelings about backyard camping, but who does have strong feelings about me being able to sleep at night). I can't give them those other parents, because those parents are busy taking care of their own kids in tents, and also because those parents are imaginary. I can only give my kids the best me. I thought that meant the me without limitations, the me that doesn't get hung up on "questionably rational" worries, the me that operates without fears and anxieties and coyote concerns. That would also be the me that pretends to feel things I do not feel, the me who hides from her truth, the me who doesn't trust herself because she doesn't listen to herself. The best me might not look like the me who chooses fun things every time. The best me might be the one who knows who she is and feels what she feels and deals with all of that first, before deciding what to do about backyard tents.

Fear and love do not live together, so I thought I had to ignore the fear. But love does not force. Love invites, and love listens. Love sees where I am, and says, *Okay, we'll start there.* Love says, *You don't have to pretend. It's simpler. Stop tying yourself up in knots and really LISTEN.*

Standing there with my feet in the dirt, all the tangled-up priorities in my heart had space to unravel. I could stop worrying about what I should do and start with what I knew. My choices had not been *listen to myself* on one hand or *do the right thing* on the other. Listening to myself was also the right thing to do.

When I said an honest *no*, I felt safer. I felt like I was being heard, like my concerns were not being ignored, like I didn't have to grab onto control—and I really didn't, because I wasn't about to smash up my own boundaries. This makes sense. Ignoring my gut is an insult to my system, and if I do it, all I learn is that I can survive the insult. But honoring my gut reminds me that I have inner wisdom. I think this is a muscle you have to work on. There's the courage muscle, for feeling fear and doing things anyway, but there's also the muscle of intuition, and for that one to grow strong, you have to practice listening.

Maybe someday I will let them sleep outside. Maybe when they are bigger than the coyotes. Maybe they will grow up to be wonder women who eat coyotes for breakfast. (Though honestly, I kind of hope not.) We can revisit the issue then.

In the meantime, patience, kindness, and vitamin D. I don't know if this is really allowed, but when I give myself permission to try, I feel a little braver.

CHAPTER 6

Through the Big
Yellow Doors

Permission to Know Who You Are

When you have to buy everything in multiples of eight (pillows, forks, fitted sheets), you find yourself at IKEA more often than you might be comfortable admitting in public.

"IKEA," said my daughter, Evelyn, when she was three. "Isn't that the place where we go and I cry a lot?" She was not wrong.

The key to a successful IKEA trip, when you have six kids, is to wait long enough between visits that you only remember the delight of discovery (Hello, useful new serving bowl!) and not the way bored children orbit around you while you shop, as though you are the planet they cannot escape, and they are your cranky moons.

Promises of checkout-line juice boxes and fair-trade

chocolate bars are not enough to overcome their strong genetic tendency toward shopping misery. I remember being a bored shopper child. I sympathize. But I survived, and now I must pass this tradition on to my own kids (though their experience of this time-honored ritual has been seriously curbed by the existence of Amazon Prime).

Yes, we could leave some of the kids in the on-site childcare center, but shopping for flatware is a useful life skill. Besides, this is family bonding time! And anyway the childcare is usually full and also playing the kind of movie that would have Evelyn climbing the walls in an effort to get away from the omnipresent, terrifying screen. (That would be *any movie*. Evelyn does not yet appreciate the cinematic arts.)

Misery-shopping is better.

I've tried listening to myself to see if that could get me out of IKEA, but all I heard was: *The plates are all chipped; it's time to get new dishes.* My psyche is not conflicted about shopping for things we need, but somehow that does not make the trip more fun.

When you finally do have to walk through the actual store, it helps to have a game plan on par with what NASA does for a moon landing. You do not want to be comparing dish options while also reminding six-year-old Eli that a bin of kitchen towels is not a ball pit, and therefore no, we cannot jump in that. You do not want to be weighing the merits of the aqua shower curtain versus the blue one while Evelyn is trying to stuff a cat-shaped throw pillow into the cart and Sadie is trying to sneak off with the stroller to play some kind of race-between-the-aisles-and-hope-you-don't-take-out-any-of-your-fellow-shoppers game. You just don't.

Dane and I keep a running list of everything we need to

stock up on, organized by where we'll find each item in the store, and synced across our phones in case we need to split up. Exact colors and amounts needed are noted. Every product description has been read and stock has been checked online before we even leave the house. We do not mess around. We are serious about inexpensive modern household goods. Besides, researching and planning gives me a sense of control over the whole trip that will be seriously lacking once we walk through those big yellow doors.

There was, for example, the time we needed new pillows for our bed. I knew I wanted down pillows, not "down alternative," so that made things simpler. I could skip the non-down aisle completely. Easy-peasy.

I should have seen my doom coming. Nothing is "easy-peasy" about shopping in a store the size of Rhode Island. My mistake was understandable: I was lulled into complacency by all my planning. The pillow section would be my undoing.

With one antsy Evelyn in the stroller, a chattering Eli in the cart, and Abigail, Owen, Audrey, and Sadie milling around me, I discovered that I was unprepared for pillow purchasing. I thought I had considered all the options (size: king, material: duck). I thought I could just grab my pillow and go. But no. When I found the king-sized, down-filled pillow shelf, there were *three* pillows sitting there, just waiting to mess with my shopping mojo. Did I want a side sleeper, a back sleeper, or a stomach sleeper pillow?

What is the difference between a side sleeper, a back sleeper, and a stomach sleeper pillow? Is one objectively better than the others? Does one have more feathers? Which one will make you wake up with a crick in your neck every morning, so you can't turn to the left without wincing? Or I guess, more importantly, which one won't?

Dane did not know what the difference was, either. "They have different labels?" he guessed. Apparently "did not know" was the same as "did not really care."

I considered turning to my good friend Google, but I was pretty sure the kids had enough patience for either "wait in line to pay," or "wait while Mom reads the whole internet," but not both.

"I'm going to have to research this at home," I said, but the panic rising in my chest came out in my voice. Researching at home meant that, for one thing, I would still have no new pillows, and for another, we would have to come back. Soon. Before we had a chance to forget how difficult it is to maneuver through the store with a constellation of grumpy almost-adolescents.

You can't just buy a thing without finding out all there is to know about that thing, can you? I think you cannot. It's not just that I have misplaced pride in my identity as the Queen of Researching Useless Things. It's that if you're willing to ask enough experts for input, you never have to make choices from that uncomfortably vulnerable place called "trust." There's always an answer if you research *enough*.

And if you've done all the reading, asked all the questions, read all the relevant studies and cross-referenced all possible outcomes, well, then even if your choice ends up being wrong, you don't have to feel guilty about it, because you did everything you could to make the right choice. Research is where I put all my anxiety over decision-making. I can just study it all away. I can break every dilemma down into smaller and smaller questions and look for the answers Out There.

"Well," Dane said as people streamed past us in search of their own Scandinavian kitchen gadgets and flat-packed cabinetry, "I am going to choose a side sleeper pillow, because I sleep on my side." That was his entire criteria: "because I sleep on my side." He was not going to research feather versus down content, he was not going to look up what would be considered "side sleeping" rather than "accidentally twisted in the blankets sleeping." (I might have accused him of having lazy shopping habits, if I had not just seen him wrestle six twin-sized blankets into the cart while simultaneously keeping Eli from climbing out.) He was just going to buy what he wanted.

It had not occurred to me that I could make a decision by choosing what was best *for me*. Maybe, if you are who you are for a good reason, you can do that. You can just pick a pillow the same way you order a deli sandwich, choosing what seems best to you, and hold the mayo. Maybe sometimes the answer is to stop looking for answers. It does sound simpler than trying to make only the best choices all the time.

I have spent several years of my life sleeping curled up on my side around tiny babies, but really, I am a back sleeper. I know this. (This might be because I once read that sleeping on your side will give you wrinkles, but I don't think so.) When it is up to me, when all I have to think about is "How do I sleep best?" and "How do I not wake up feeling like someone has been poking me in the shoulder all night?" I sleep on my back, every time. Apparently there are special pillows for that.

It turns out you have to listen to yourself even in the small stuff. I thought you could save that for the big things, like where to live and what to devote your life to and whether to let your preteens sleep in a tent in the backyard and even whether to make the IKEA trip in the first place, but no. The small stuff is where you practice. The small stuff is where you build up a habit of listening to yourself, so that when the big stuff comes around, you already know what to do. You don't want to have to wonder, when you're listening for direction about the things that might change your life, whether the voice you're hearing is your own. If you practice on the pillows, you'll already be familiar with the sound of your own voice. You'll know your own self.

And anyway, not every decision is final. Sometimes you are limited by the sheer number of dollars, minutes, and brain cells required to make a decision, and that decision can't be made twice. Other times you can find a way to replace the Swedish pillow if you buy the wrong one. Sometimes you just have to try a thing and see what happens and save the energy you would have spent researching for other stuff, like getting everyone buckled back into their car seats instead.

In the bedding aisle at IKEA, my children were looking for a reason to start a pillow fight. This is the downside to display models: someone might actually use them.

"Are we done yet?" Sadie asked.

I took a deep breath and put away my phone. We were so done. I was done with this particular shopping trip (we wouldn't discover that we'd forgotten to buy drinking glasses for at least another hour), I was done being circled by my sweet vulture-children, I was done thinking about pillows. I was done trying to make the perfect choice. There is no perfect choice. There is outer wisdom, and there is inner knowing, and the balance between the two is a dance I am still learning, like a backwards waltz in high heels where I keep tripping over my own ball gown. I was done. Research means answers are out in the world, and some are. But some answers are inside, even small, silly ones about bedding. Sometimes you have to stop asking questions.

Sometimes you have to be still and listen. You already know the answer.

I hefted the pillows into the cart. Dane bought the side sleeper, I bought the back sleeper, and I still don't know what the difference is between the two. I think we all slept better not having to wonder.

CHAPTER 7

The Risk of Yoga Pants

Permission to Show Up Anyway

I am not into public yoga. I am barely into yoga on a mat in my bedroom. I do try, though. I fire up a yoga class on YouTube (which I think of as a *private lesson*), I do what the instructor says, and I sweat in the privacy of my own house. I also answer back to the screen, because I imagine that the YouTube yoga instructor and I have that kind of relationship.

She does not correct my poses, and this may be a downside to the Doing Yoga in Secret method, but: silver lining! No one ever tells me I'm doing it all wrong! I will take that, because I do want to be strong and centered and connected to my body, but I'm . . . not. At least not yet. And I don't necessarily need a whole group of strangers in expensive workout clothes to know this about me.

This is not only because of the wobbly tush problem, but okay, maybe it's because of the wobbly tush problem. The *wobbly tush problem* is what happens when you wear yoga pants, or at least when I do. It's a physical manifestation of my inner wobbly feelings. That's why I never wear my yoga pants out of the house. In yoga pants, there's nowhere to hide. You just walk around all wobbly for the whole world to see.

Yoga pants get a bad rap, I think. People talk about wearing your yoga pants out in public like it's not impressive, like they're just the default uniform for those of us who can't be bothered to find pants that button. But I don't think that's right. I think yoga pants are brave. (I mean, yes, they're easy to wear, too, but that's a bonus.) Yoga pants say: *This is me, just as I am, with no sparkly distractions. Either I trust you to understand that I am sharing a precious gift with you—the gift of me being me—or else I don't care what you think. Either way, my pants are an expression of inner wisdom. Here I am. Just me. Nothing else.*

I'm not there yet.

I'm still in the stage where I see everyone else in yoga pants and think: *Great! Cute! Comfy!* And then I see me in yoga pants and think: *Hmm, I will wait on the stretchy clothes. I will save them for someday, like maybe a day when my tush is already toned.*

My friend Leigh is the kind of yogi who practices on the beach at sunset. I imagine she does fancy yoga things like *knowing her left from her right* and *not falling over when she practices*. A couple of times, she's led a class just for our friends. I've watched. It looks like fun. Everyone else looks like they know what they're doing. No one else wobbles in their yoga pants.

At the end of those classes, Leigh walks from mat to mat while her yoga-people lie with their eyes closed in Exhaustion Pose. (I'm a little fuzzy on actual pose names. My YouTube yoga instructor does not get annoyed with me about this.) While they're all lying there, Leigh leans over each person and gently adjusts their head and shoulders. The adjusting looks delightful. I would rather do this than the yoga, honestly.

So when I heard that Leigh was planning another class, I decided to go. One hundred percent reason for going: the adjustment thing. I actually spent time thinking about this. Could I say, "I'm not into public yoga! I'm wobbly and uncoordinated. I just want the adjustment part"? I thought I could not. The adjusting was a reward for enduring the public yoga. No minor embarrassment, no soothing touch ritual. That looked like the deal to me.

I was definitely going. That part I had decided. I tried on my yoga pants. I felt like I was wearing pajamas. I put on my jeans. I felt like I was headed to somewhere other than yoga. I put on the yoga pants again. I took off the yoga pants again. Yoga pants plus adjustment, or jeans plus nothing? Relaxing ritual in pajamas, or dignity without human connection?

I settled on the most complicated solution possible. I did not skip the class. I did not wear stretchy workout things. Instead I rolled up my mat, I put it in the car, and I wore the wrong pants. I drove off in jeans and sneakers and no yoga clothes. I don't know what I was planning to do.

By the time I arrived, Leigh had begun unrolling mats in one corner of a big room. In another corner someone else was setting up a journaling station with pens and paper and what looked like writing prompts. In the middle of the room was some kind of found-art collage-making setup that I could not quite comprehend. More friends with normal-person yoga clothes arrived and started rolling out their mats on the floor all around me. I rolled mine out, too, and kicked off my shoes, figuring I could melt into the journaling group at any moment if needed.

Leigh stepped onto her mat a minute later and explained the yoga plan using words I did not really understand, so I made my best peaceful yogi face and nodded. "If you need to take a break," she said, "just lie down on your mat and practice your yoga breathing." I don't think she even gave me any side-eye. Everyone else stepped onto their mats. They all looked comfortable in their skin. They were just here to get *better*, maybe. They were fine-tuning themselves. They were becoming Advanced Enlightened.

It's hard to show up when everyone else knows what they are doing and you're still trying to figure stuff out. It's especially hard when all of life is like that. How are you supposed to make a difference in the world when you don't have anything figured out yet? I flopped onto my yoga mat to breathe.

That is when I realized I did not have any yoga breathing skills. I should have researched yoga breathing before I came! Too late now. I would have to do regular breathing, like with air and stuff. I hardly even know how to do *that*, honestly. How do you make your breath fill up your belly? Mine always wants to live in my chest.

Maybe breathing is something I should hold off on until I learn how to do it, like public yoga. When I know what "lion's breath" is, then I will exhale. When I'm fit, then I'll try group yoga. When I'm centered and normal and not-anxious, then I'll get to know some people. Until then, I should just keep my wobbly tush at home, I'm pretty sure. But how was I supposed to *get there*, to that wonderland of self-improvement? I hadn't figured that out yet. And I was starting to worry that I was not really earning the end-of-yoga adjustment thing. I did not have my breathing all together! Oh my gosh, I couldn't even relax properly.

I lay there breathing-not-breathing for an eternity or maybe only fifteen minutes; I'm not really sure. The journaling people were still at their tables, doing things that did not look scary at all. The art-making people made their art. And I remembered I was supposed to be resting and being present with my breath, not being jealous of how easy it looked to be the people in my peripheral vision.

The yoga folks who were still standing did their last yoga-flow thing (I was not kidding about my relationship with all the pose names). Some of them had joined me on the floor and were lying serenely, breathing nourishing breaths and wearing the right pants. Not that I was comparing myself to the people in my peripheral vision again ten seconds after remembering that wasn't a healthy choice. (Yes, I was.)

Leigh invited the last yogis standing to go ahead and lie down, too. She showed us how to signal if we wanted to be adjusted or not, and then she stepped into the rows of mats to do her thing.

Out of the corner of my eye, I watched her move from mat to mat. (Yes, I am addicted to my peripheral vision, what do you want from me?) At first, I was checking to see if maybe there was a secret adjusting password or anything I should know before my turn. There was no password. No secret handshake. I watched Leigh lean down again and again. I saw her really see each person and offer them a moment of connection just because they showed up. She did not grade their yoga efforts. She did not say to anyone, *You know, you did not earn your space on the mat today.* She was just present with them, one at a time, as though each one was the only person in the room.

Maybe, I thought as I watched her, *maybe I don't have to get everything in order first.* I am the way I am for a good reason, and maybe I don't have to get everything right before I can belong. Maybe it doesn't even matter which pants I wear.

Lying on my mat, I took a deep breath, fresh and new. You can't hold onto your breath, you know. It comes, and it goes, feeding us as it comes in and cleansing us as it goes out. It doesn't stay, but it always comes around again. Whether we're paying attention or not, it comes around again. It's life practice. We don't have to learn from it if we don't want to, but we do have that option. We have the option to pay attention. I can choose to notice that the air I just breathed out might be the air you breathe in next. We're all connected, whether I believe it or not.

I don't have to get everything together first. Maybe I don't even have to know the real names for yoga poses. Maybe I don't have to wear the right pants, and maybe I can if I want to. I don't have to hide my wobbly self. We are connected because we're all breathing on this earth together, not because we all have equally firm yoga bodies.

And if I don't compare myself to the person on the mat next to me, I won't even know if I don't measure up. That is not such a bad strategy. No one else was comparing me to the person next to me. No one else was paying any attention to me at all. I was the only one measuring me against an invisible yoga ruler and deciding I wasn't good enough. I was the only one making me feel unacceptable, which meant it was, annoyingly, up to me to fix it. Who had to accept me for me to feel acceptable? Who had to decide that I was okay and allowed before I would believe it? If feeling acceptable comes from being accepted, well, I always have the option of accepting myself as I am, already loved, already made in the image of love, wobbly tush or no. If

I accept myself, I get to feel acceptable. It's exactly that simple *and* that complicated.

Yes, I'd rather wait to be seen until I'm more presentable but getting comfortable with the truth of who I am—and where I am on my yoga pants journey—is simpler. I think that means I can bring my wobbly self wherever I go. I don't think I have to learn to choose the yoga pants, but I don't think I have to avoid them, either. I'm pretty sure it's okay to need what I need and to be where I am, and it's okay to grow into a bigger, braver person, a person who is not afraid of public yoga and stretchy pants.

When Leigh came to my mat, she did not say a thing. If she had opinions about how I showed up, she did not mention them.

I closed my eyes and she placed her hands on my head, then moved them to my shoulders, creating gentle pressure, reminding me to be here, in my body—even if the truth was that I didn't feel ready. Even if the truth was that I didn't know what I was doing. Even if the truth was that I felt a little ridiculous, no matter which pants I wore.

She just met me where I was. Which is, after all, the only place I can be.

CHAPTER 8

Pressing the Pause Button

Permission to Be Here Now

I thought I knew how the day was going to go. I had a list, and it was full of things like "make a grocery list," and "return the shoes that don't fit," and "write the thing," and "schedule appointments." This wasn't a comprehensive list, obviously. This was the important stuff I didn't want to forget. Everything else— get someone a string cheese, find the missing sock, slice the apples, braid the hair, replace the pen caps, put the wet towels in the dryer, hunt for the scissors, wonder how I got to be in charge of all these things—was implied. I didn't know where a person would find a piece of paper big enough for *that* whole list, so it lived in my head. There were more than enough things in there to fill a day. Or six. Once, when the kids were going to stay at my friend Sarah's house, she told me not to worry about leaving them because she knew what to do. "I've seen how you do it," she said. "You just never stop moving."

That's what I thought the day was going to be like: full and packed with predictable details. Then a wild bird flew in through the front door.

This has happened before. I don't know what makes birds think our house might be a good place to visit, but every few months one flies in to scout us out. The last time it happened, we didn't see our new feathered friend right away. We heard him, but his chirp sounded remarkably like the smoke detector. We just figured one of our safety devices had a dying battery or something. (In retrospect, this is probably something we should have investigated even if we didn't have a history of wild birds flying into the house.) It took us hours to realize that the smoke detectors were all fine, and in fact, there was a bird perched on the edge of one of the second story windows, peering down at us as we ate dinner. Dane had to climb up there to shoo him out.

This latest bird, though, was not disguising herself as a smoke detector. She flew from windowsill to windowsill, trying to get back to the bare trees and scrubby bushes she could see outside. The kids looked at me as though I might know what to do.

I started giving orders, because that seemed like the next right thing.

"I'll open all the outside doors. Owen, you go left. Audrey, you go around to the right. Sadie, you stay here. No one get between the bird and the door! No blocking the exits!" I was making this up as I went along in the hopes that my confidence would trick the bird into thinking I was in charge. "Okay, bird!" I said firmly. "We're going to shoo you out now!"

The ceiling over our living room is vaulted, with windows near the ceiling to let in more light. The bird flew back and forth between those windows, far out of our reach. "When they go low, I go high," was this bird's motto.

"Now what?" Sadie asked, because the bird was clearly not interested in our surround-and-push-toward-the-door strategy.

Five minutes later, Owen was on a ladder, Abigail had closed all the doors to the bedrooms, Audrey and Sadie were looking for anything that might reach the higher windows (a broom?), and Eli and Evelyn were sitting behind me on the stairs, watching the show and hoping someone planned to provide popcorn. Someone did not.

I thought the day was going to involve watercolor paints and subsequent spot-removal for a size four Elsa dress. I did not bargain for this.

We waved our arms and pointed at the door. (The bird was unimpressed.) We took many photos, because why not? We found a blanket and tried to use it to kind of whoosh the bird toward the door, but gently, so we wouldn't freak her out. (The bird cocked her head as if to say, "I am a bird, and you are not a matador. What do you think we're doing here?")

"I don't think this is working," Owen said, as the bird flapped her wings against another window. How do you convince a feathery creature that she would be happier if she flew through the opening in the wall instead of into the plate of glass? I do not know how to speak bird.

"Is it lunchtime yet?" Evelyn asked, because four-year-olds do not care that much about "I'm already doing seven things, hold on."

"It is not," I said. "It is bird time." Thirty seconds later, I realized that was the wrong thing to say, because now she is going to ask me every day until forever how much longer until bird time. *Is bird time before or after morning snack time?* I couldn't wallow in my rookie mistake, though, because the bird suddenly flew down to ground level. We held our breath as she hopped along the back of the couch, and then onto the throw pillows, and then onto the armrest closest to the front door.

"Out," I whispered. "Out you go!"

The bird hopped up . . . and flew *into* the door.

Well, crap.

I inched closer to where she had thumped down, in the little wedge of floor space between the couch and the open door. I was going to . . . ask her again to leave? Take another picture? I'm not sure what my plan was, but suddenly, somehow, the bird squeezed through the gap between the doorframe and the hinges, and she was free.

"She's out! She's out!" Evelyn sang.

"That was great," Eli said. "Can we play a board game now?"

We could not, I was going to say, because I needed to get back to all the things I meant to be doing before spending half an hour on bird patrol, but—

"Uh, Mom?" Owen was still standing on the ladder. "There's bird poop everywhere."

Of course there was.

We found paper towels and cleaner and a trash bag and more paper towels. Abigail helped me move the couch and take all the cushion covers off it to "wash," and by "wash" I mean "disinfect while trying not to gag."

Twenty minutes later, I told Owen to put away the ladder so I could get back to work, but—

"Uh, Mom?" Owen was behind me. "There's more bird poop in here."

I had already forgotten that the bird had looped through the entire downstairs part of the house, swooping through the living room and family room and dining room and kitchen. Why am I in charge of remembering where she flew? Why am I in charge of bird poop at all? I did not invite that bird into my house! I wondered if we could take a cleaning break. I wondered how likely it was that our neighborhood birds had any kind of bird flu in their systems. I found more paper towels.

This is what happens. There are a lot of things to pay attention to at once, and if you don't, you will end up with bird poop in your living room three days later.

Unless the thing in front of me is urgent—a lunch to make, a bird to shoo—I'm never really sure which details to pay attention to first, but as long as I'm doing *something*, at least you can see I'm trying.

And I figure if I keep moving, no one will notice that I don't know how to get it all together on a deeper level than the level of bird poop. Life would probably be simpler if I could, but I don't know the next steps. Or the first steps. Or any steps. Having my life together is a secret code that I have not cracked. I might be the wrong species for this; I don't know. I mean, maybe I'm just not the kind of person who gets it all together in any meaningful way. Tending to details feels like a reasonable substitute.

Plus, handling those details makes me feel more competent than I am. It's like a tiny little declaration: *I know how to order the socks!* Am I good enough now? Am I worthy of this life? Yes, it's complicated, but what else am I supposed to do?

Even on bird-free days, I am always thinking three steps ahead of what I'm doing, just to keep my life from flying into chaos. When I'm driving, I'm thinking about where I'll park.

When I'm going to bed, I'm thinking about getting up in the morning. When I'm singing, I'm thinking about the next line in the song, so I don't get lost along the way.

That one is also partly because music is not among my gifts. I cannot naturally follow a melody. If I don't pay close attention, I end up sort of humming and flapping my arms to a beat no one else is hearing. Clapping along would undo me. It's a challenge.

I do try, though, because if I keep trying, maybe I can at least get it all together for the length of a song. I don't really make progress, but it's better than shooing birds out of the house, at least.

This is something I can practice on the Sundays our family attends church. (It's a side benefit of going to church, sure, but a pretty good one.) On one of those Sundays, I sat down in my very fancy folding chair with Evelyn on my lap to wait for the music. I did a quick headcount to make sure we hadn't lost any of the kids, and to be sure the younger ones had snacks to hold their attention if nothing else did. I was ready. I was paying attention. I was going to follow along. The band started playing, and I looked up—but instead of moving from one verse to the next, they left just four lines up on the screen. We sang that verse over and over and over, sinking into the lyrics.

I did not have to prepare to sing the next part because there was no next part. I could focus on those few words, turn them over in my heart, let them wash over me again and again, and it was enough. It was a kind of meditation, singing that one small piece. I let the truth of the words settle on me, seep down into my bones.

But really, the point wasn't the words. The point was the *rest*. The point was that for one moment, there was no work for my body or my brain. Just: rest. Just: be held. Be present. It was a little moment of letting go, of starting fresh, and that is precisely what I needed.

I relaxed into my chair. My mind stopped racing ahead. My thoughts slowed. What if this was what it really meant to have it all together? What if having it all together means your mind isn't racing ahead, so your brain and your body are in the same place at the same time? Maybe *together* is about your heart and your mind, your body and spirit, all holding together, all present and seen and heard and felt. Maybe having it all together is when your heart is dancing along with your feet.

Sitting there, I felt like the beach when the tide goes out— not empty, but lighter, no longer underwater. The tension in my chest eased up. I realized I had been holding my body tightly to keep all the details together—as though the details were stored in my muscles, and I had to stay tense to keep from dropping all the balls. The tide went out, my arms relaxed, nothing fell. I was safe. This was unexpected. It was almost as though I did not have to hold all things together. The truly important details—the sun rising, gravity enduring, the universe sustaining carbon-based life forms—were being held by something deeper and wider than me and my mind and my abilities. The world kept turning without me having to make it happen.

I sat and was refilled, the tide coming back in. My what-to-do-next list had washed right out of my consciousness, but energy was pouring back in, energy for the details that really did matter. I wonder if resting makes it easier to remember why they mattered in the first place.

This—resting, being here and now—felt right. It felt like a reordering. It felt like my whole self coming back together, like bringing all my parts back to love. That's all I had to do to get it together. I just had to stop running and spinning and juggling and bring my whole self back to the truth: that I am the way I am for a damn good reason, that I am loved as I am, that I *am* love, that I am connected to all the love in the universe. Details are just details. Bird poop is just bird poop. It doesn't mean anything about my head or my heart.

I thought getting it together meant always knowing what to do and how to be. I thought it meant having a plan and never questioning yourself, but it's simpler than that. Togetherness is about bringing all your parts back together and being fully yourself. Whole. The details aren't part of it; the details are separate. I'm not sure what to *do* with those details yet, but when I have all of my self together, maybe they won't matter so much. Maybe I'll just handle them as they come.

I had to hold still to come back together, letting my brain slow down so my body and spirit could catch up again, so I could be on the same page with myself. No wonder I never had it all together, if I could never stop and rest and think and feel, if I was forever chasing out the birds and chasing down my days. Resting in the truth of who I am—and who I do not have to be—is simpler than trying to look like I know what I'm doing. Rest is where I start to see the shape of myself. It's where I discover what remains when motion stops.

This is the invitation. Not to keep running, but to rest. It sounds like: *take notice*. It sounds like: *be filled*. It sounds like: *enough*.

CHAPTER 9

That Means You're Doing It Right

Permission to Un-Meet Expectations

"So . . . what do *you* do for fun?" The woman standing in front of me was trying to make small talk, which is difficult under the best of circumstances, but at that moment I was trying to hold three-year-old Abigail's hand on one side while keeping baby Owen from crawling away on the other. This was what I did for fun. This was also what I did for survival. At that stage—trying to figure out how to parent very small children with no real sense of whether you're doing anything right or whether the ground will ever stop shifting beneath your feet—it's enough.

My attempts at communicating this came out sounding like, "Oh, well, you know, uh . . ." so she turned to Abigail. "What does your mommy like to do?"

Abigail squinted up at this friendly, if unfamiliar, woman.

She took exactly zero seconds to think about her answer. "Sleep," she said.

This was true. This is still true. What would I like to do in my free time, if I had free time, which I do not? I would like to sleep.

It's strange, how many fewer hours there are in the day for things like sleep and play and *I don't even remember what else,* now that you're an adult. Kids' days seem to go on forever, with long mornings and lazy afternoons spent climbing things and claiming to be "bored," because there is "nothing to do" in this house full of art supplies, board games, LEGOs, dress-up clothes, decorative Band-Aids, and kid-powered vehicles.

Meanwhile, my grown-up day is full, and not full of skateboards and watercolors. Somehow "journaling" doesn't seem so important next to a mile-long grocery list and a clothes dryer that has decided it no longer wants to spin. Adults are allowed to do fun stuff, theoretically—it just has to wait until all the other stuff is done. Which it never seems to be.

Even if I'm not trying to hold everything together, there's still a giant checklist that grown-ups have to get through every day: plan the meals and make the meals and clean up after the meals. Check that the floor is not covered in crumbs/dust/hair/confetti/dirty socks. Vacuum the floor when it turns out to actually be covered in crumbs/dust/hair/confetti/dirty socks. (Again.) Reply to the email. Do the work. Figure out why the phone has stopped receiving text messages. Read up on current events. Move the laundry. If you have children, bathe and dress them, or at least encourage them to do those things themselves. Shoo the children out into the fresh air and sunshine. Mediate squabbles. Keep track of whose turn it is to hold the flashlight.

Yes, you have electric lights. No, that is not relevant to the flash-light situation. I know the details are just details, but there still are a lot of them.

I've never been *good* at all of this, but I have always been aware of how I fall short and have the polite sense to be embarrassed about it even as I'm trying to get it all done.

I always figured that *afterward*, after I'd conquered the whole complicated Grown-Up Responsibility Checklist, then, in theory, I could move on to doing the things I secretly wanted to do. That was how I would give myself permission: when everything else under the sun was done, then I would move on to the things that made me come alive.

I do not know who made the Grown-Up Responsibility Checklist—we can call it the GRC for short—but either they had more than twenty-four hours in their day, or else they were planning to sell me something that would give me more than twenty-four hours in *my* day, because I cannot do all these things in the amount of time it takes for the earth to spin around on its axis. (Possibly whoever came up with this plan was from another planet, one farther away from the life-giving warmth of the sun.)

And anyway, the GRC is not a to-do list. It's a what's-expected list. It's waking up every morning and earning the dollars and keeping the house from falling in around your ears and maintaining healthy relationships and being a force for good in the world while also making sure everyone in your sphere of influence is fed and clothed and well-adjusted. And it never ends.

The confusing thing is that having a plan—knowing what's expected—should make life simpler, shouldn't it? You don't have to wonder what matters. You can just *do the next thing*.

But what I feel when I'm trying to get through the whole

Grown-Up Responsibility Checklist is less "satisfaction" and more "burning shame"—because completing that checklist feels like the minimum requirement for being good enough, and *I can't do it.* I do not get a "job well done" feeling from wrapping up that plan, because I never wrap up that plan. More things are constantly being added, actually. It starts with the basics—keep everyone alive, do your work, vote—and just keeps growing. Put away the clean clothes *before* they're all full of wrinkles. Reply to all the email and all the text messages and the direct messages *and* learn to check your voicemail. Make phone calls, on the actual phone. Come up with a meal plan that fits your lifestyle and palate and budget. Make a budget. Keep your life crumb-free. Learn to use a curling iron. The more I learn, the longer the list gets. Read good books. Look for growth opportunities. Ask hard questions. Find time for contemplation. Practice being centered and staying grounded. Teach my kids conversation skills, even though I have none whatsoever. And now I have "rest" on there, too. I want to make sure to rest, so I can bring all the parts of myself back together again.

But if rest helps you come together, what makes you come alive?

One day, when our kids were smaller, my friend Abi came over to drink tea with me in my kitchen while the littles ran wild in the backyard. Abi is a writer and an artist, and she is much cooler than I am. She knows things. I said something about the dishes in the sink, because mentioning them at least feels like an excuse for not having done them, and because "dishes" feel like a reasonable stand-in for "all the things you might have expected me to do that I have not, will not, and probably cannot do." The "dishes," you know, are never-ending.

Abi shrugged. She did not care about the dishes. She once had a mentor, she told me, who had a philosophy about dishes. "You'll never regret the dishes you didn't do," he'd said, "but you'll always regret the paintings you didn't paint."

I didn't actually want to paint anything, but regret? Regret I understood. Regret is the cold rock in the pit of your stomach when you realize something important has been lost. Regret is the gripping tightness in your chest when you see that the important something did not simply slip away, but you dropped it. Regret is discovering that you let go of the gold to hold on to the dust, too distracted by fear to chase after hope.

But I knew what would happen if I stopped trying to clutch that dust between my fingers. The voices in my own head would start whispering about what people would think: that I was lazy, that I was irresponsible, that I was depriving my family of my time and attention. That I was being selfish. People would think I didn't understand the rules. I would look like I didn't have my life under control—and I'd have to keep going anyway, no matter what other people might think.

It's the "no matter what other people might think" part that's hard. Ignoring the laundry is not especially difficult: you just look the other way. Turning off the voices that nag at you about how *leaving towels in the dryer forever isn't a solution*? That is the real trick. Those clear expectations sound so much like simplicity—but when you're working toward meeting someone else's expectations instead of your own, that is when things get complicated.

Other people's expectations of you are like the universe: they're continually expanding and hard to fully comprehend. You can get lost in there.

When I started practicing with this "let go of the dust" plan, the first thing I discovered was that when you choose your own priorities, it shows in your life. People will notice. Most won't care, but some will say things like, "You haven't returned my email. Do you know you haven't returned my email? Did you even see my email?" and "What is *that*? Is it a laundry mountain?"

They will notice. That means you're doing it right.

That's why ignoring the Checklist feels so scary. It felt like forfeiting my spot at the table, where I wasn't sure I had ever been welcome to begin with. It felt like taking off a covering, a skin, that was never actually part of me but kept the wolves out.

To ignore the Checklist is to bare your soft belly. (At the very least, someone is going to give you suggestions on how to get hard abs.) Meeting expectations is so much more comfortable. If there's any risk, it's the risk of failing to follow all the rules, which is far less scary than the risk of revealing your heart.

You can never really meet all those expectations, because you're only aware of some of them, and they're also subject to change without prior notice. (It's in the fine print.) In exchange for trying, though, you get a heaping basket of regret about the things you never did because you were too busy being respectable.

I never had time to watch the kids ride bikes because there were couches to vacuum under and messages to check. I never sat down to write because there were groceries to shop for and lost keys to find. I never told Dane what I really wanted because there were tomorrow's lunches to pack and that new calendar app to check out.

No matter how much we like to pretend we can multi-task our way to superhuman, *the hours don't stretch.* And if you keep trying to do everything on the Grown-Up Responsibility Checklist FIRST, you'll never get to anything else. Ever.

It seems like there's a right way and a wrong way to spend your time, I know. It seems like the GRC is the responsible plan, and anything else is selfish.

My friend Kate told me something about selfishness, though. Kate is equal parts spiritual and fierce, and you can tell just by looking at her. She looks as though she has walked right up to the thin places in the world, the places where the veil between spirit and matter is so sheer you can almost reach right through, and now she walks around holding on to the edge of that curtain. She was also a pastor at the church where I first heard Jessica speak. Kate says that selfishness is the belief that you are a self, separate from all the other selves walking around on this earth. When you believe you're separate, who knows what you might do. Selflessness isn't self-denial, Kate says. Selflessness is when you understand that *there are no selves*. You aren't a separate self, or at least you aren't *only* a separate self. You're also one part of the whole. So is everyone else. We're all in this together, quite literally, breathing the same air, animated by the same spirit, and sharing the same elements that will forever be recycled among us.

So me coming alive was not an either/or proposition. Coming alive was not selfish, and the GRC was not selfless. This was not about choosing between my needs and my family's needs. I'm part of my family. I'm part of the whole. I don't need to prove myself before I can be myself. I do not have to choose between feeding my soul and feeding the world. Feeding my soul is part of feeding the world. This is both/and.

I am the way I am for a good reason—and that includes the things that wake me up. That includes everything that brings me joy. That includes everything that makes me ME. I am this way on purpose. Me.

Bringing *me* back into the picture simplified everything. When I started asking what I needed in my life, my priorities started to shift. Or maybe they didn't change—maybe asking the question clarified what mattered to me all along. It brought the truth of who I was back up to the surface, the truth that I was not built to live according to someone else's rules, and that meeting other people's expectations took a ridiculous amount of work. It brought up the truth that I cared about some things—like each of us being who we really are, and everyone having what they need to flourish—more than others—like figuring out what shoes are in style this season or cleaning the kitchen counters on a regular basis. It just kept bringing up more truth.

So then what was I supposed to do with my Grown-Up Responsibility Checklist? The email did not magically start answering itself. The laundry did not condense into smaller and smaller piles, like a rock turning into a diamond under pressure. And yet . . . I could not meet expectations and meet myself at the same time.

So this is how you un-meet expectations, then. You say no. You throw out or give away all the stuff you're tired of organizing. You let the laundry pile up, or you tell everyone to wear those jeans one more time. You get slow at replying to email. You delete stuff. You delete more stuff. You give yourself permission to do what you need to do, and you don't wait for anyone else's approval.

I started asking myself, *This thing in front of me, this thing that demands my time and attention, is it feeding my family? Is it feeding my soul?* And if the answer was *no*, I let it go to make room for something that would. I let the Checklist go unchecked, and I didn't regret a thing.

This is a new valuing of yourself. Refusing to follow the rules, letting the dust blow away in the wind, speaks for itself. It says, *I am worthy of taking up time. I know I haven't earned it, and the thing I produce might not be impressive enough to justify the time it took, but it made me wake up. It made me come alive.*

And that is worth everything.

CHAPTER 10

The Distraction Is in the Details

Permission to Turn Off the Spotlight

Everyone knows beaches are fun and relaxing. At the beach you're playful or you're resting. You unwind. You let go of the tension of your daily life and groove to the rhythm of the waves. Everyone knows that.

Everyone also knows the beach is a little bit peculiar because we're basically all walking around in our underwear and pretending this is perfectly normal. *Yeah, no, I'm cool with just sitting here on the sand in what amounts to spandex undies. This is not uncomfortable or strange at all! Just sitting here with my bathing suit and my body issues. I'm fine.*

My body shape is known as "stretched like a rubber band that is almost ready to snap but let's hope it doesn't," mostly because of that whole growing-six-babies-one-after-the-other thing, but my body works hard, and I like it. We're a good team, my body and me.

I also like my rash guard that looks like a T-shirt for swimming. I wear it with mismatched swim bottoms, as though I throw on any old thing to go to the beach, as though I'm here all the time. I am almost surfer chic, sitting in my beach chair with sand scraping the backs of my thighs.

There's sand everywhere at the beach, of course. That's what the beach is made of: warm expanses of beautiful, sparkling sand. Sand like a surprising, gritty seasoning in your lunch. Sand that gets into your car and your shoes and under your swimsuit in the most uncomfortable of ways.

You get to sit there on the sand, hot and sweating and wondering how long until you get a sunburn—but personally, I hardly notice these minor discomforts because my real job at the beach is to keep the ocean from swallowing any of my children. I barely have time to compare my body to the bodies of the beach volleyball players or the bikini-wearing sunbathers.

Did I say how relaxing the beach is? Maybe I should have left that part out.

It's all good as long as you stay zoomed out on the big picture. The big picture is the waves, the shore, the blue skies, the umbrellas, the smiling people with their eyes closed as they lay on their towels, the splashing children with their multicolored suits. Yes, in the big picture I am still in my beach chair, my eyes darting wildly, constantly counting heads. Yes, in the big picture it is still true that I forgot my flip-flops and wore my sneakers to the beach. And yes, I packed a lunch and forgot the water bottles. But you only *see* that if you zoom in.

Up close you would see that my makeup—which I have to

wear for sun protection, obviously—is melting off my face, that my hair is frizzing up in the damp ocean air, and my skin has the bluish tint of a person who does not bask in the sun very often. Some things are best kept at a comfortable distance, is what I am saying.

It's hard to say why I don't go to the beach more often.

The last time we were there, sitting in our sandy little chairs, Dane offered to rub sunscreen onto my exposed parts (of which there were not many—remember, rash guard like a t-shirt). Dane burns if he even thinks about the sun too hard, so he started in on the zinc oxide as soon as we hit the sand. I burn less, and I would rather touch sunscreen approximately never, so I had skipped it. But Dane still had more on his hands.

"Want me to get your arms?" he asked, like a reasonable human being.

I hesitated because yes, I did want him to put sunscreen on my arms. I did want that. No sunburn, without having to touch greasy white stuff that I wouldn't be able to wash off? Sign me up. I just didn't want to call his attention to my really weird arm hair, and if he was going to rub my arms out in the open, in the sunlight, he was going to have to look at them. He was going to notice. It would be like shining a spotlight right on them. The trouble with a spotlight is right in the name: it lights up all your spots. It shows off all your blemishes; it highlights all your stains. I would prefer a wide view and soft light. A couple of filters, maybe.

A spotlight is supposed to highlight something worth looking at. It's supposed to be the star of the show. So what do you do if something less glamorous comes into the light? What do you do if it's all eyes on your imperfections? If I have to be in the spotlight, just *standing* there doesn't feel right. It feels like I should be juggling and doing magic tricks, trying to direct your focus away from my less admirable parts and toward my more impressive ones. *Look HERE! Not THERE!* Maybe I could keep some parts out of the spotlight and shove others in, and that way I could manage your experience of me. I could control your reactions, or at least let myself believe I could. I can just chop myself up into easily digested, bite-sized pieces for your consumption. And apparently, I'd rather do that than avoid a sunburn. This is how you take care of other people's opinions of you rather than taking care of your own self.

We're all doing it, in different ways. The beach volleyball players are showing us their athletic selves, but maybe they're not talking about their emotional selves or their selves that are worried they might be wasting their weekdays behind the wrong desk. The sunbathers are showing us their tanned shoulders and their posh sunglasses, but maybe not their secret longing to be silly and splash in the waves. We're not faking, but we're being pretty freaking selective about what we reveal. What will happen if we step our whole selves into the spotlight? We don't know. That's the problem. So we manage what you see and what you don't.

If you think you have to manage yourself around your people, you never fully relax. You're constantly reminding yourself that you're not secure. Maybe you're not really good enough. You never know. You never know what they would say to your whole self. You never know if you could be seen and known and loved anyway. And you can't invite anyone else's whole self into the light while you're still hiding yours. Hiding encourages hiding, and showing up in parts does not feel like living in wholeness. If you stay in pieces, you always have to wonder if maybe the next piece to hit the spotlight will be the one that will turn everyone away. Maybe my arm hair will be the thing that makes people grimace and shudder—and as long as I keep hiding it, I'll always have to wonder and worry. There's always something to be afraid of until you step into the light. Then at least you'll know.

This is where trust comes in. I like to think I'm waiting to show myself until I trust the people around me, but what I really want is to trust that I know exactly how they will react. It's not quite the same. I don't have to know what will happen to know I need to be seen. Yes, it's riskier than waiting until I can be sure of the outcome. But that's the way it goes.

And there was Dane, still holding up his sunscreen-covered hands.

"Yes," I said nobly, as though I was volunteering to lead a mission to save the world from an alien invasion, as though this was an act of self-sacrifice. "I just didn't want to draw your attention to my really weird arm hair, that's all."

He looked mystified, probably because he was. "What's weird about your arm hair?" he asked.

We'd been married more than fifteen years. If he hadn't noticed, I wasn't going to explain. I closed my mouth and held out my arms. (It's nothing, really. It just grows in all different directions, like a hedgehog that needs a hairbrush.)

He rubbed sunscreen on them without recoiling in horror or even making any faces at all, and then he kissed the top of my head, which was still sunscreen-free.

Nothing happened. I don't think he could even see the spotlight. Are there people who would look at my whole self and make fun of me? YES. For sure. But good news: I don't have to be married to them!

We're all out here dancing in and out of the spotlight, contorting ourselves into what we think are pleasing forms, and other people can't even see the stage. It's like they're wearing sunglasses. Maybe they're looking the other way. Maybe they're hiding from their own spotlights. No one cares, and even if they do, you can't let that get in the way of being yourself and living your life. The admirable parts *and* the embarrassing parts all come together to make up the whole of you.

The Franciscan priest, Richard Rohr, says that when we finally give up on fixing ourselves, when we finally accept that the goal isn't to solve all our problems but to learn from them, what we find is "the rediscovery of an authentic and original power, where human clay meets divine breath."[1] We are invited to be our whole selves, problems and all. Not only that, we're invited to be our whole selves *with other people.* "All created things," he says, "are a mixture of good and not so good." That's just part of being human.[2]

I might still have sand in my armpits and my hair may be tangled forever from that wind, but hey, at least I won't have to weave myself around an imaginary ideal, and I won't waste my energy trying to control other people's minds and hearts. I am not nearly flexible enough for that. Instead I can focus on things I can control, like whether I remember to bring all of my kids home from the beach at the end of the day.

And anyway, maybe it doesn't matter. Maybe letting the tiny details (or arm hairs) get in the way of health and wholeness (and sunburn protection) isn't the best plan after all. Here's a simpler idea: step into the spotlight, or turn it off and walk around in the plain old light of day. Let people see you. Then you'll know. And you won't even have a sunburn to remind you of what you were hiding.

CHAPTER 11

The Impossible Discipline of Rest

Permission to Drop the Ball

People say bizarre things to parents. This is just a fact of reproducing. The more kids you have, the more uncomfortable the conversations become. If you have one kid, you get a lot of, "Will you have another one?" and "Ready to start trying for number two?"

If you have at least two—and especially if you have at least one boy and one girl—the go-to question switches to, "Are you done yet?"

Someone once told me that after you have four kids, it doesn't matter how many more you have—it's all the same amount of work. This is a lie. I have six: Abigail, Owen, Audrey, Sadie, Eli, and Evelyn, and I would just like to say that keeping them all fed and alive takes exponentially more effort now than when there were fewer of them. Just keeping them in clean underwear and fresh sheets is pretty much equivalent to tap dancing up a mountain, in terms of energy output.

Right after Evelyn was born, I was put on bed rest for recovery purposes. For weeks I had to avoid all strenuous activities, like answering the front door, or sitting. All I could do was lie in bed with a newborn swaddled on my chest and a pile of blankets on the rest of me.

I was totally up for this, at first. Just me and a squishy-soft newborn. Just me and this baby whose head smelled like heaven and water. Just us. Nothing to do, nowhere to go. This was good, because I did not have the strength to move the blankets that covered my body anyway. All we could do was lie there all warm and safe and cocooned.

(New babies are a little bit like cats. They want your complete attention, even while they sleep. It doesn't take a lot of thought, just a lot of presence.)

Just me and Ev. But Ev mostly slept through this whole period of our lives, so it was pretty much just me, alone with . . . me.

The funny thing about recovery is that if it goes according to plan, you do, after a while, start to recover. Which meant more of me, alone with me.

No meals to plan and shop for and cook. No email to check, no projects to work on. No other kids to tend to. (They were around, but they had more interesting adults on hand, ones who could fold paper airplanes and take walks around the neighborhood and also sit up.)

Just me.

And as I started to feel stronger—eventually, I could move the blankets without help—I started to wonder what I was doing there. I felt like, if I could move the blankets, I should. If I could stand up, then lying down was just lying down on the job. That's kind of what *lying down on the job* means. I felt like there was something I was supposed to do, and I wasn't doing it. Whatever it was.

One minute I would be lying there thinking: *This is nice! Just me and my lovely baby, staring out the lovely window into the lovely trees* . . . And then the next minute I would think: *But wait, what am I supposed to be doing right now? It feels like I'm supposed to be doing something. This doesn't feel normal. Tap dancing feels normal.*

It is one thing to not be busy. It is one thing to hold still so you can come back together. It is quite another thing to be alone with yourself, unable to move, for hours and days and weeks.

When you're alone with yourself, there are no distractions. Nothing demands your attention. You do not have the experience of time slipping away while you tend to one urgent thing after another, from morning until night—but all those little things that made up a day gave me a sense of normalcy. If I had things to do and they were the same things every day—even if wasn't the whole Grown-Up Responsibility Checklist—I never had to ask myself what was next or why I was doing some of those things at all. Normalcy is its own kind of distraction.

And if I stopped doing all that and was left with a gaping emptiness—what if it never got filled back up?

So I let things start sneaking back in. I started with the stuff that I loved and missed, the things that fill my soul and make me feel whole. Still lying down, mostly, I let the kids bring me their drawings to admire and their books to discuss and their skinned knees to kiss and their conflicts to solve. I took pictures of Evelyn lying beside me. I wrote down the things I wanted to remember and the things I didn't want to forget, which is almost the same but not exactly.

And then I thought I would check my messages, just for a minute. Why did I do this? Everyone who needed me already knew how to find me. Everyone who needed me was already in my house. And still, I checked.

My inbox was just full of normal things, but they kept rolling in, with requests and suggestions and deadlines attached. Could I put this on the calendar? Did I want to sign my kids up for that program? Could I come up with something for this project? Could I send over a quick picture? Could I just reply about this one little thing?

Of course I could!

Those pings meant that I was not lying down on the job, even if I was mostly lying down while I answered them.

I could do one more thing and one more thing, even though I was supposed to be doing zero things. All the things I needed to do were stay in bed and take care of Ev and drink herbal tea.

These are the things I wanted to do. These are the things I cared about more than anything else in the world. And instead I kept creeping out of bed to send off a reply to this or that, because people were waiting. Because I had said I would. Because it felt normal.

This is how I came to be balanced on a step stool, trying to snap a "quick photo" to add to a social media share of an article I'd written, when Evelyn started to fuss. "Quick photos" are not actually quick—possibly because I have no particular photography skills—and I only had a few minutes left before the afternoon light ran out. There was not time to nurse and change and settle Evelyn and get back to the photo. And I stood there on the step stool, leaning forward with the camera, *hesitating*.

Baby, or photo? Photo, or baby?

I started to unravel, until my heart caught up with my brain and started shouting: *Who am I? Who does this? What am I even doing here? Am I the person who can be counted on to hold on even when the rope is pulling her over a cliff, or am I the person who lets go? What is even on the other end of that rope?*

My friend Colby, who was also a pastor at Kate and Jessica's church, says there are two kinds of energy in the world: there is love, and there is fear. (Sadly, he did not tell me this until Evelyn was a toddler.) You could think of them as voices calling out to you all the time, and you get to choose which one to follow. There's the voice of fear, telling us that we're not good enough, that people won't like us as we are, and that we're not really worthy of love and belonging and all that good stuff. Then there's what he calls the voice of the Spirit, and that voice, he says, is always leading us toward becoming our best selves. The voice of the Spirit sounds like an invitation to become more fully alive. I know exactly what he's talking about, because I can hear those voices right in my own heart. I hear the loud, insistent voice of fear all the time, but when I remember to listen, I can hear the still, small voice of the Spirit, too. It's the voice of love, reminding me—reminding us all—of who we are and who we were made to be. So which voice am I spending my days listening to?

Some of the things I did every day were because I remembered who I was and who I was made to be. Some things were part of my day just because they made me come alive. Some were! Listening to my kids, moving my body, making space for creative work, staying up late into the night with Dane after the kids were asleep—these all fed my soul. But that still left a whole lot of other things: following the news, tidying the house yet

again, answering messages in a timely fashion, scrolling, scrolling, scrolling, checking out that new website or market or nature
trail or green juice bar—all the things I did to keep up, which
is a fancy way of saying I was still afraid of what would happen
if I didn't do them. I might be forgotten, for one thing. I might
be left behind. People might think rude things about me. I was
afraid I would drop the ball and that dropping the ball would be
evidence that I was never worthy of holding it in the first place.

Mindless routines, the ones that are "just the way we do things,"
the ones that don't grow out of any particular intention—checking
messages before you even brush your teeth in the morning, signing
the kids up for yet another round of lessons and sports and practices, renewing memberships we never use, settling in for another
night of Netflix and ice cream, and one more scroll through the
phone before bed—I think are always, ultimately, driven by fear.
Sometimes it's the fear of being left out or left behind. Sometimes
it's the fear of rejection, or the fear of disappointing people, or
the fear of being different. Sometimes it's just the fear of looking
deeply at yourself. That's how all those things made it onto that
Grown-Up Responsibility Checklist in the first place.

If the voice of the Spirit is calling me toward who I was made
to be, and my daily life is pulling me in the other direction, well,
no wonder it felt like I was sliding off a cliff.

The best thing about the voice of the Spirit, though, is that
it *isn't* the opposite of the voice of fear. It isn't even playing on
the same field. They're not pulling at opposite ends of a rope,
waiting to see which one can knock you over first. When the
voice of fear calls you to walk one way, the voice of the Spirit
doesn't tell you to run the other way—it tells you to step out of
the lane entirely.

When the voice of fear tells me: "Don't disappoint people! No one will love you if you disappoint them," the voice of the Spirit doesn't say, "Disappoint as many people as you can. Hurt everyone's feelings; that will be awesome." The voice of the Spirit says: "Stop using other people as your reference point. You're loved just as you are." Right?

When the voice of fear says, "Keep up! Don't be left behind or forgotten, OR ELSE," the voice of the Spirit does not say, "Pfft. Sit down on the side of the road and pull a blanket over your head already. Disappear." The voice of the Spirit says, "Do what you are here to do. Create what you are here to create. There is no left behind. You cannot be forgotten. You're fine. Keep going."

When the voice of fear says, "You only matter when you're doing good things. You're only worthy if you're serving someone else," the voice of the Spirit does not say, "Oh yeah, that's true." And it does not say, "Ugh, quit helping other people, would you?" The voice of the Spirit says, "You matter because you *are*, not because of what you do. You matter because you were made to be like this. You are who you are for a good reason, and you can do whatever you need to do. Just show up as your whole self in the doing."

The voice of the Spirit looks at the this-or-that mentality of the voice of fear and says, "Well, that's interesting, but here's a third way."

This is helpful, because sometimes the right choice is obvious, but often it's not. If I'm trying to take a photo to avoid disappointing someone on the internet, and my baby is also crying, I pick my baby. The photo does nothing for me. Holding the baby pours life into my soul. (Your mileage may vary.) But most of the time, Evelyn wasn't going to cry. So what was I supposed to do with myself during all those other minutes?

Most of the time, I kept moving so I didn't have to face the fear that I really might not be enough just as I was. Facing that possibility scared the crap out of me. It was physically painful to hold still and wait to see what happened. But if it was true—if I really was okay just as I was, right then and forever—there would be no more need to tap dance. Ever. On the other side of that terrifying look in the mirror would be freedom, if that were true.

The stuff I had been doing—checking email one more time, answering another message, saying yes and yes and yes when a simple "no" would do—all the stuff that called to me when I was doing nothing? That was filler, and it was filling up scary, empty space. So all I had to do was replace the filler with . . . nothing. Not with something more important. That would be easy. If you have a choice between the right thing and the wrong thing, you usually choose the right thing. But when the choice is between the wrong thing and nothing, well, sometimes the wrong thing doesn't seem so bad. Sometimes it seems important to have something there. The universe seems to want to fill in all available space, including the space in my days—but maybe I didn't need to let it.

Watching Evelyn sleep, I didn't have any answers, so I started asking questions all over again.

I asked myself, *What is most important to me right now?* Most important was being where I was, with Evelyn, whose newness would fade so quickly—spindly fingers replaced by chubby ones, new-baby smell replaced with the chamomile of baby soap. Resting and healing were important, too, to find my way back to strength. Learning to listen was important, if I was ever going to figure out why it was so hard to be here, now.

I wanted to stay put and stay present, so I asked myself, *What does now feel like?* I had so much practice being in my head, in the past or in the future or juggling details, that I was barely acquainted with right now. I had to actively notice to see what *now* was like. Now was warm and bright, with sunlight pouring in through the windows and falling onto the foot of the bed. It was a breeze ruffling Evelyn's feathery hair. Now was aching and heavy, but also solid and snug. Now was so beautiful and would be gone in an instant, and if I closed my eyes, I might miss it all. I cried exactly as much as you might think, noticing what now felt like.

And then, looking at all of that, I asked, *What is the next right thing to do?* Not the next thing. I can come up with a thousand next things without even thinking. The next *right* thing. If I get quiet and listen, the still, small voice inside me rises up with one answer. What I would like is a Next Right Life Plan with a clearly marked path, or at least a brightly illuminated end goal. What I usually get instead is enough clarity to see one step ahead of me on the path I'm walking. Sometimes I know where the path is heading. Usually I don't. I get just enough light to see one step forward, and then I wait for the next step to appear. Lying there with Evelyn, I would hear: *Take a nap.* Or: *Ask Dane to bring you a salad.* Or: *Go sit on the balcony in the sun awhile.* They were small things, but they were what I needed. They were answers no one else could have given me, because no one else knew exactly what I needed next. That isn't anyone else's job to know.

And when I was feeling really brave, I asked, *Why don't I want to be alone with me?* You have to be careful with this one, because you'll get an answer. I didn't want to be alone with me because I was afraid I'd find out I really was the worst. I was afraid to be alone with me because there was a whole lot of stuff I'd been avoiding looking at, like whether I was a good-enough mom, and what hard conversations I needed to have, and whether I needed to change things that would be easier not to change, like the ways I buried conflict and the things I said to myself when no one was listening.

But holding space for the questions also makes space for the answers. And once you hear your own answers, once you look in that mirror, you don't have to be afraid of it anymore. The empty space I had been trying to fill, that was the space between me and my questions. It was the space between me and all the things I was afraid to look at. But being able to look right at the truth without looking away—that felt like simplicity.

When I crawled back into bed with Evelyn, the blankets didn't feel so heavy anymore, and neither did the quiet. I could almost hear the voice of the Spirit whisper: *Just this. Just this.*

CHAPTER 12

The View from Above

Permission for Imperfection

Evelyn wandered over to where I sat tucked up in the corner of the couch, staring out the window and stalling instead of making dinner. "Mom," she said. She looked concerned. I prepared myself for an explanation of who had taken whose LEGOs, or maybe a monologue about which snack she wanted but could not find.

"In a play?" she said. "You know, when there's a grown-up person on the stage? How do they *also* pretend to be a kid person?"

These are the kinds of questions that were not in the parenting training manual.

"I bet they use robots," she said thoughtfully, before I had a chance to explain about *makeup* and *costumes* and *using your imagination*.

There are a handful of things the preschoolers in my life can be counted on to gravitate toward. Explanations that seem reasonable only when you're three feet tall is one of them. Bubbles are another, especially if there's a chance the bubble solution will accidentally be spilled on my shoes. Another perpetual hit: food in surprising shapes, like star-shaped sandwiches, or spaghetti, which can be twisted up and is longer than food really should be. I make a mean spicy tomato sauce, too, but I have never yet convinced a three-year-old that spicy tomato sauce is, in fact, food. At three, Evelyn was a spaghetti-loving monkey who would take her noodles plain, with olive oil and salt and no annoying flavors to get in her way.

But still, she would eat it, so I would cook it. I stood in front of the stove one evening, waiting for the water to boil while she wrapped her arms around my legs. Luckily, I can make spaghetti equally well with or without the use of my legs. I salted the water, tore open the package, and slid the noodles into the pot. Without untangling Ev, I reached for a long-handled fork. I knew from experience—much repeated experience—that if I didn't separate the noodles, they would come out in disgustingly chewy strips of two and three noodles stuck together. I would not mind proving myself wrong occasionally, but in this case, the noodles were sticking together already.

I swirled and stirred and cursed under my breath a little, but the noodles were not interested in my plans. They would not separate.

When my kids are learning to do a thing, they tend to point out the obvious: *I can't do this. I don't know how.*

I also point out the obvious: *You don't know how to do it—YET.*

"Life is not a test. Life is for learning," I tell them, because that is what parents are supposed to say, and also because I happen to believe it.

"Yet" is always a possibility. Where you are right now has very little to do with where you will be a month from now, or a year from now. You are not where you want to be—yet. But you can get there. This is what I say to them.

To myself I say other things.

"Why does this always happen?" I asked no one in particular about the spaghetti. I understand that the noodles might prefer not to be eaten, but still. I feel like they've made their point and could get on with the business of cooking without sticking.

The noodles had other ideas.

"Oooh!" said Evelyn, still wrapped around my left leg. She could see the noodles as I lifted them out of the pot with the fork, hoping steamy air would help them want to unglue themselves from their neighbors. (I may have made a noise like an angry pirate at this point.) "You're making ska-betty!"

For a while, the older kids tried to correct her on this one. "No, sweetie, it's *spaghetti*," they would say, drawing out the word the same way you would toss a ball to a toddler, slowly, to make it easier to catch. *Spaaaaa-ghettttt-iiiiiii.*

I always stopped them before she could catch on. Mispronounced words are a good portion of my daily joy in life, along with wind chimes, a secret stash of chocolate, and kids who say things like: "Okay, Mom, you're the dinosaur and I'm the teacher. Wait here," and then hand me an eye patch and run away.

Ska-betty is adorable. We don't need to correct her; she'll figure it out eventually. She'll outgrow this phase. In the meantime, it's charming, and I need something to distract me from the stuck-together spaghetti noodles that signal my own failure and incompetence.

Have I ever tried to fix this spaghetti problem, by the way? No, I have not. I have just practiced doing it wrong one million times. I have never even asked Pinterest for three easy tricks to make whole wheat noodles not stick together—which you know Pinterest has, just waiting for me somewhere in the bowels of its smartfeed of solutions.

I like to think I am still growing, and that is true. But growing does not mean that eventually I will become the Spaghetti Master. There is no guarantee that I will, ultimately, get good at all the things, or even at this one thing. There is no guarantee I will even get *better* at all the things. And even if I do get better at *some* things, there will never come a time when I have figured out *everything*. I used to think human development was like a journey up a mountain. You learn more things; you reach another summit. Eventually you have learned all the things from all directions, and you reach the top. Congratulations, you are now good at everything! Or you are at least good at everything that matters to you, everything you've been practicing and learning and working on. You have reached the pinnacle of humanness, and you can stay there until you get lifted up to heaven, which should not be too arduous a trip because you're already pretty close.

Except that is not how it works. Some things I have to keep relearning, over and over again. Some things I do not get better at. Some things keep being hard. The more I learn, the more clearly I see how much I do not understand, how much I may never understand. We are not climbing the mountain to all-knowing competence, we are crawling around on the ground, following a path through the grass, and it's not entirely clear where the endpoint is. All we know is which direction to head, and sometimes even *that* is murky.

Some days, we stand tall and see everything all around us. Other days we are up to our knees in mud, slogging through a ditch and trying mightily to believe there is something better up ahead. Every once in a while, we get to the peak of a little hill and think we've achieved something marvelous. But it's really all just part of the path. The path is not leading you to a place of being more perfect and knowing all the things. It's leading you to know yourself better and to understand more about the *nature* of things.

Which means I might never learn to cook the noodles properly. If I never get this right—if I never grow out of the sticky-noodle-cooking phase of development, if my noodles stick together until the day I die—what then? What does that mean?

The noodles were taunting me, I was pretty sure, willfully clinging to their noodle-buddies so they could stay partially uncooked and wear out my family's chewing muscles. Evelyn did not seem disturbed by this, down there on the floor where she wove her body in and out between my ankles like a giant hairless cat. "Is it ska-betty time yet?" she asked.

I will always think three-year-olds and their spaghetti words are adorable. From up here, they will always be charming. If they mispronounce things until the end of time, I will be delighted. I will never correct Ev when she asks for "instruction paper" for all her crafting needs. It sounds much tidier than its alter ego, construction paper, even if it's actually the very same thing.

Which makes me wonder: how must my own well-meaning mistakes look from a higher perspective? Because there's always a higher perspective, isn't there? I bet no one is looking down on me thinking, "Ugh, she lets the noodles stick together at least sixty percent of the time. How about we just smite her now and be done with it?" (It might be more or less than sixty percent; I don't know. It's not worth the math to figure it out. The smiting is the point here, and I think it's unlikely.)

Do I really believe that baby mistakes are cute and kid mistakes are learning opportunities, but my adult screwups are a final judgment? Is there an expiration date on grace around here?

From where I stand, I should have more skills at this point. I should be better at this. I should be amazing at noodles. But there is always a higher perspective than mine. There's always more to see, so there's always a better way to understand. I used to think I was climbing a mountain, and now I know I'm actually pressing forward through uneven terrain, reaching out for the people around me as I go. Perspectives shift. Worldviews expand. Mine is just stuck on the level of noodles at the moment.

But if the goal of the journey is not to learn how to do everything perfectly—if the goal is to learn about yourself and the world and the divine in the doing—what is the spaghetti trying to teach me? What have I learned?

I have learned that I expect myself to get things right all the time. I have learned that not knowing how to do a thing feels scary, because I assume the not-knowing means something terrible about me. I have learned that I act as though smaller people deserve more grace than bigger people, which is to say I've learned that I haven't been listening to the voice of love on this one.

I have learned that some things do not come with practice, at least as long as you keep practicing the wrong way to do them. I have learned that sometimes you have to try a new plan if the one you have tried a million times still does not work. There is no need to try a million and one times. Either try something else or be happy with what you've got. That was my first mistake—I was refusing to do either. I was trying what I had always tried and expecting something different to happen so I could finally be good enough—but nothing different was going to happen. Expecting spaghetti to make me good enough was my second mistake. Making good noodles does not actually mean a whole lot about you. Maybe it means that you paid attention to something you were taught; maybe it means you were resourceful in finding solutions; maybe it means you were open to experimentation and tried a variety of techniques before finding the right method. The fact that I continue to be terrible at noodle-cooking might mean I am still a beginner chef, feeling my way forward without a plan. But it says very little about my worth as a human being.

From another vantage point, maybe my attempts at life look less like "disappointing failure" and more like "endearing bumbling." Maybe I am not supposed to have it all figured out. Maybe I am Evelyn, only a few decades later. Those decades are nothing, just tiny blips of time.

Accepting that I will never prove my worth with a pot of spaghetti—accepting that this is not even what spaghetti is for—is simpler than living in perpetual disappointment over the nature of my humanity. Accepting that my perspective is not the highest one is simpler than expecting myself to become something I was never meant to be. The wider, truer perspective looks more like love and less like smiting. The invitation, when my perspective bumps up against that one, is to try adjusting to that wider, truer view, bringing it into my life and into the world.

Maybe eventually I will look back and see how far I've come and be amazed. Or maybe I will realize the distance isn't even the point. I don't know whether I will have cracked the sticky noodle code or not, but I do know that how I think about it will be different. Twisting myself into knots over the starchy nature of noodles is not actually serving anything.

"Is the ska-betty *finally* ready?" Evelyn asks, as I drain the noodles.

And it is.

The noodles are not perfect, and I am not perfect, but they are done, and for today, that is all we need them to be.

CHAPTER 13

This Isn't about You

Permission to Know Your Assignment

All of my favorite grocery stores have sample stations set up to encourage snacking while shopping. One has trays out in the produce section with slices of oranges or chunks of melon piled on top. Another has a counter in the back corner with little nibbles of things set out in tiny paper cups. I do not love the sample station for myself. I love the sample station because it is the opposite of bored-child misery shopping. I prefer to save misery shopping for occasional trips to bigger stores, not experience it every time we hit up the produce market.

When the kids know there are samples coming, the refrigerator case is not "freezing and awful" and "are we done yet?" because they are anticipating what will be at the other end of the aisle. They're wondering: will it be fruit and cheese? A new juice? Bites of chia bars? It could be anything. It could also be Swedish meatballs, which they will not want, but if that happens, their parents will probably agree to buy a string cheese or a box of sweet potato crackers as a consolation snack.

If a store can keep my children happy while we shop, I will be a customer for life. That's just the way it goes. Sorry, boring stores. This is my reality.

During one of our frequent grocery store trips, I pushed the cart over close enough to let Evelyn reach for a cup of strawberry beet juice off the sample counter, and the other kids all chose little paper rounds holding crackers with cheese squares on top. "Have you tried these?" the woman behind the counter asked me. "You should. They're delicious!" The cheese was spicy, she said, and creamy, and I think she said something about saltiness? I didn't catch it all.

"Thank you!" I said, but I did not pick one up. I needed to say no, because I couldn't eat dairy, or grains, or sugar, or really any of the other things on that counter at all. My body rebelled during my last pregnancy and developed a whole bunch of food sensitivities that did not go away, so—assuming I didn't want to spend the next couple of weeks with my midsection puffed up like a painful balloon—I could basically eat nothing but vegetables and lemon water. It was a delightful situation. (Except it was not.)

"No, really, you should!" the woman behind the counter said, trying to encourage me to lighten up and indulge a little. I knew I needed to pass. I could not pick up that mini-plate of snack foods, no matter how drool-worthy its contents might be. It was just really hard to say no because *she was the cheese expert.*

And she did say *should.*

Should is my kryptonite. Anytime anyone tells me I should really look into something, or listen to that one podcast, or consider this other life philosophy, I hear that as an assignment. It sounds so official. "You should . . ."

I figure I probably should.

If I were keeping a running list of things people told me I should do in a given week—which surely I would not do, because that doesn't sound like a healthy choice, but let's just say IF—that list would be as long as my twelve-year-old's hair. Twelve-year-olds can grow hair longer than they can reach to brush. I would not be surprised if I woke up tomorrow and Audrey's hair was down to her knees, long enough to tuck into the tops of her boots. And my list would be longer than that.

The librarians think I should sign my kids up for the summer reading program, because they know my kids love books and sticker rewards almost equally.

My friend Amelia thinks we should pack up our kids and meet at the beach, because it feels like that kind of day.

My friend Grace texted me that we haven't seen each other in ages (true), and we should get together for tea (maybe also true).

A stranger on the internet thinks I should read the new novel she loves, and I am sure she is right.

Some of our friends are hosting a dinner, and there's still space around the table; they think Dane and I should join them.

The ads on my phone tell me I should see a new movie I've never heard of (not to mention buy a sundress and a new necklace to wear, and then stop for coffee afterward—my phone can give me a whole evening plan in one scroll through Instagram).

It goes on. And on. If you're trying to meet everyone else's expectations, I guess "should" makes that a little bit simpler—you don't have to guess what people expect if they straight-up tell you. "Should" makes those expectations super clear. So convenient! Except I know that trying to meet outside expectations makes my life more complicated. Every minute I spend trying to live someone else's version of my life moves me farther away from knowing who I am and what I need. That's why I was trying to let go of expectations in the first place. If you let go, what do you do with all the *shoulds* that keep coming your way?

You should check out that new grocery store.

You should look into that program for your kids.

You should consider this new exercise routine or meal planning service or record-keeping system or social network.

You should join that group and take that class and also check out that website.

You should sign up for that event. You should come with me!

You should, you should, you should.

I'm never going to get to all the *shoulds* because, for one thing, the space-time continuum does not allow for that possibility. (Trying to outwit the realities of space and time is another definition of *complicated*.) Even if I could, most of those things will not actually make my life better or happier or simpler or more fulfilling. But I will still investigate every single one of them, because *should* feels like an assignment, and I have always been a good student.

I'll even research things I already know I don't want to do. Someone could say to me, "Instead of bathing your children, you should really have them licked by goats," and I would sit down and research all the reasons that goat spit is not a substitute for baby soap, just in case it ever comes up in conversation again.

This could be a full-time job, and it's not even a job I like. Or get paid for. I was talking with my friend Carrie about this the other day, about all the things I could be researching for every one of my kids, all the things I should be checking out and then maybe doing, for myself, for my marriage, for my family, for the world. I felt like I was falling behind, and I hadn't even committed to anything. Carrie had been researching all the options for kindergarten for her kids, so she knew what I was talking about. "It's hard to learn all the things," she pointed out. "It's a big responsibility. It's overwhelming, and honestly, it kind of sucks."

(I may be paraphrasing.)

But Carrie is wise, and Carrie is right. Considering every life option anyone else ever thought of makes my already-full head spin.

I know that every person you meet has something to teach you, but maybe that's not the same thing as letting someone assign you a research paper every time you meet up for a cup of chai.

I'm only doing it because everyone else's choices are probably more valid than mine. Someone else said I should do something, and all the someone elses are better at being a person than I am, so they're probably right. Or at least they're probably more right than I am.

But investigating every option there ever was keeps pulling me off my own path and onto everyone else's paths. It yanks my attention here and there, left and right, twisting backward and leaning forward. That's not a life—that's a puppy running wherever it's called, distracted by anyone who knows its name or holds up a chew toy, leaping in every direction until it ends up peeing in somebody's shoe.

Brené Brown says she tells herself, "Don't shrink. Don't puff up. Stand on your sacred ground."[1] That is her authenticity mantra. That is, in other words, what authenticity looks like. It looks like standing in the truth of who you are and what you know to be right. Authenticity does not look like following up on every idea anyone else drops in your lap.

But it still feels kind of iffy to say, *I already have a purpose and a plan, and your idea doesn't fit. Thanks, anyway.* Wouldn't that be rude? To listen to my own intuition instead of to someone else's strong opinions about my life?

The opinion-givers always sound so much more confident than I feel.

But investigating all those opinions is denying my own wisdom, ignoring my own sacred ground. If I am the way I am for a good reason, I need to be that person, not follow in the ways of all the other people.

So what do I do with all those *should*s? Do I just ignore them? Is that my most authentic choice?

At home, I pulled Kelly Corrigan's book, *Tell Me More*, off my shelf. "This book," I read, "is about things we say to people we love (including ourselves) that make things better."[2] These are, Kelly writes, the hardest things humans have to say to each other. One of those things is, "Tell me more." [3] It's not "Tell me what I should do," or "Let me tell you what YOU should do." It's not "Let me tell you why I am uninterested in your advice," either. It's "Tell me about that," and then nothing else—just quieting down and listening. It's harder than it sounds.

I've always found this to be helpful in conversations with my kids, who have a lot to say. They mostly don't want me to do anything in particular with their words; they just want to be heard. They want me to listen. They want me to hold their stories. That's the work of being a parent, once they're old enough to zip their own sweatshirts and open their own granola bars, but maybe it's not only for parenting. Maybe *just listening* is the work of being around other people.

I'd been hearing "you should . . ." and thinking it was a list of things to do. When I started listening, though, I discovered that's not what it was at all. When someone said I "should," they were really trying to tell me something about *themselves*, something about what they choose or what they love or what they want to see in the world.

When I heard "you should," sometimes it really meant "I love," or, "I want to." Or sometimes it meant, "I'm being brave and trying something new, but I feel alone, and I need support."

"You should read this book," meant "I love this book."

"You should try the cheese," meant "I think it's tasty."

"You should take this class," meant "I like the idea of this class."

"You should take that leap," meant "I dig calculated risks."

"You should come, too," meant "I am nervous about going."

"You should check out that new gym," meant "I want to try that new gym, but I'm afraid or I'm stuck or I think I'm not the kind of person who checks out new gyms, but maybe if we both do it, I will be more comfortable."

Yes, sometimes—coming from people who know you well and are always and forever *for you*—*should* means something else, something like, "Here is a gift that will make your one and only life even more marvelous."

But most of the time, when someone says, "you should," I'm convinced they are not trying to give me a to-do list. They're giving me a message about their own feelings, and all I need to do is listen.

Listening—to myself, or to whomever is talking—is a sign of respect. It's a very quiet way of saying *you are loved*. It's the listening, not the reacting, that says *you matter*.

There's no love in chasing down all the *should*s. When I do that, I haven't really seen you, I've just let you knock into me, your kinetic energy sending me off in a new direction. But I am not a ping-pong ball, and your *should* is not a paddle trying to smack me onto a new path. And if I listened to *myself* more, I might feel less obligated to chase everything someone else thinks I should chase. If I spent more time listening to myself, I might know if a thing was right for me without having to investigate it at all.

When someone says, "you should," I am trying to hear, "share my joy." If that doesn't work, I try to hear, "please encourage me."

"You should" isn't about me; it's about them.

I don't have to *do* anything at all. If "you should" is about the other person, then just listening is enough.

I can say, "I want to hear more about that! Tell me everything." I can listen. I can just listen. It's so much simpler than I thought. I'm not falling behind; I'm right where I'm supposed to be. This is it. This is all I need to do. My real assignment is to listen, to learn, to love, and to make my own best choices by knowing myself.

I don't have to feel guilty. I don't have to explain myself. I don't have to research anything. I don't even have to pretend. I can listen and be love.

I can say to the cheese experts, "It's good, huh? It looks really good," and then we can both move on with our lives, shining a little brighter because we connected.

CHAPTER 14

How You Know
You're Human

Permission to Be Real

I am not exactly proud of this, but I spent most of an afternoon staring into the flame of a pillar candle. I would like to say I was meditating or doing something else equally enlightened, but the truth is, I was staring. It just felt really necessary to keep pressing the sides of the candle in for an optimal burning situation. And then there's the gathering up of any dried drips and dropping them back into the molten middle—this is important and responsible, almost like recycling. I recommend the light-a-candle-before-sitting-down-to-work strategy for anyone who needs to avoid accomplishing, well, anything really, at a desk. You just light the candle there next to you, and then you have a built-in distraction whenever you need it, which will turn out to be ALWAYS now that you've provided yourself with one. (This is never how I *intend* to spend my time when all the kids are out of the house, but it is what happens.)

Every once in a while, I would pick up the candle and swirl the wax around to try to even it all out, which seemed sort of useful, right up until I swirled hot beeswax onto my right wrist, over my left thumb, splashed it onto my desk chair cushion, and dripped it onto the leg of my jeans. And of course, you can't just set aside waxed fabric to deal with later. You'd really better stop and handle that right away.

This is why I was standing in my underwear in my home office in the middle of the day, ironing the inside of my jeans onto an old towel. *Because stain removal is a big responsibility, people.*

It also explains why my lunch consisted of a handful of roasted sunflower seeds and a square of raw chocolate. Actually—no, that has nothing to do with the candle; it's just another example of where I am in my adulting skills. I have achieved Level: Ignores Molten Wax Safety Precautions and have unlocked Bonus Level: Snacks for Meals. At one point in my childhood, I thought I might be a ballerina/artist/doctor when I grew up, but instead I am ironing-in-my-underwear lady. I'm afraid I might be an imposter grown-up.

The other night at dinner, Eli showed us how he'd learned to pull a penny from his ear.

"Yep," Owen told him, "that's how they make pennies. It's somebody's job to sit at the penny factory, pulling coins out of their ears all day long."

When you are seven and your big brother is a teenager, you get to endure many things.

"Really?" Eli asked.

The rest of us nodded, because we all love a good story, and sometimes the things we imagine are better than reality, anyway.

Eli was asleep in bed before Owen realized we'd never told him the *other* way pennies are made, the way that involves an assembly line and a coin press. The way that is grounded in, you know, reality. A real grown-up would have remembered that, right? A real grown-up would make sure her kid knew the truth before bed. *Don't let the sun go down on your nonsense*, isn't that an ancient proverb?

The evidence points to: imposter grown-up.

I have been practicing being more myself, because I am who I am for a good reason, so I might as well be that person. If I'm not going to be myself, it seems like a lot of wasted effort went into making me. But the more I practice being myself, the more I realize I have not arrived anywhere that looks like completion, and isn't an adult supposed to be a complete human? Isn't adulthood the end of the growing-up road? But I'm still a work in progress. It feels like I took a wrong turn somewhere along the way.

When I was little, I assumed being a grown-up mostly meant not having to clean your room. (I didn't understand that being a grown-up meant doing it anyway.) But adults are also supposed to know about all the things they need to do, like how to choose a healthcare plan and when to defrost the refrigerator. Or if they don't know, they at least know how to find out. I don't even know where to start looking most of the time, and I'm afraid to ask because I think I ought to have the answers already.

I don't know how to organize things, like a meeting, or a march, or the off-season clothes. I don't know how to do things like stick to a routine, or figure out what time to leave the house, or convince the bank to spell my name properly. I've asked. I don't even know how to stop running out of sandwich bread. (These kids will eat it all, no matter how much I buy.)

This is my general sense of my life and myself: *I don't know what I'm doing.* Maybe it doesn't make me the worst, but it's still an accurate description of my reality.

I can't make quick decisions—I think I'm still looking for permission to make the choices I want to make or guarantees that everything will turn out well and that I won't run out of energy or get hungry along the way.

I'm never sure—what's worth pushing yourself for? When should you follow your own lead, and when should you stretch yourself? I like my couch, and I also like naps. Why go out?

I always worry about saying yes—am I accidentally double-booking myself? Have I forgotten anything important? Will I be glad to have done this, or will I regret it?

"What's for dinner?" the kids ask, and I wonder if "ennui" is *for sure* the wrong answer.

Sometimes I feel like I'm a fish that someone pulled out of the bay, flopping on my side on the pier, wondering what the hell is going on and where I fit and how I get into that ocean that I can sense is out there but can't see. I'm flailing, basically. I'm not flailing in secret anymore, but I'm still flailing. Grown-ups aren't supposed to flail, are they? I thought that if I stopped hiding, if I put down my shell, the flailing would magically go away—but it didn't. I still don't know how to follow all the rules, and getting better does not appear to be in my skill set. If I can't figure it out, if I can't fix it and won't hide it—then what? Do I just stay broken?

I told my sister Ryleigh about the penny/ear situation, which felt like a minor but telling parenting fail. Having been a younger sibling herself, though, she was unconcerned.

"Just leave it be," she said.

Just leave it be? Don't worry about it? Don't write myself a note to find an instructive penny-related YouTube video tomorrow? Don't wonder how many other parenting mistakes I made today but have already forgotten about? Can I do that?

"At some point he's going to wonder about the rest of the coins," she said.

This was a good point. There is always more truth to discover, and not just about pennies.

I asked Jessica about this a while ago, about wholeness, and whether she thinks we're broken. Is this the truth we're here to discover? Are we supposed to be looking for wholeness?

"Have you thought about what you mean by 'wholeness'?" she asked.

I had not, really. I guess I assumed "whole" meant complete, and complete meant finished, done, polished. Arrived. I believed I was supposed to have arrived, and I hadn't. I thought I was supposed to follow the rules, and I couldn't. That felt like brokenness.

"I think there's a difference between *wellness* and *wholeness*," she said. Emotional wellness looks like being happy and well-adjusted and liking yourself. She said you might not have wellness, for any number of reasons, but that isn't the same as not being whole. And she said wholeness doesn't always feel especially *well*.

Jess suggested that wholeness is about being a whole, integrated self—pulling together the parts you're proud of *and* the parts of yourself you'd rather forget about. The work—the process of wholeness—is to keep uncovering those shadow parts and integrating them into the fullness of yourself. You're already whole—you already possess all your parts—and you can work on becoming more aware and integrated and maybe even more well.

"It feels like a mystery to me," she said. "I think we are whole, *and* we can work on living into our wholeness."

If that is true, the problem isn't that I'm flailing. The problem is that I think I'm not supposed to be. *Of course* I haven't arrived. Learning to live into that kind of wholeness would be a forever journey. We will always be works in progress. I think Jessica is right: the problem isn't that I'm broken; the problem is that I didn't understand what it meant to be whole. That distance I feel between where I am and where I want to be—that's the distance between fear and truth: the fear that I'm not okay, and the truth that I am the way I am for a damn good reason.

If I'm expecting wholeness to look like always-being-well, or like perfection, well, then, of course I'm going to feel broken. Of course I'm going to believe I need something more, something outside myself to become whole. But you are a whole self. I am a whole self. We have everything we need to live in wholeness: love, and the ability to listen and to learn, and to bring our inside selves—the good and the embarrassing—out into the light.

Living in wholeness, then, would come back to allowing your outside self and your inside self to be the same self. It would look like accepting all your parts, acknowledging them, bringing them all into the whole of you. The good, the bad, the healthy, the flailing. Not hiding anything. It doesn't look like perfection, or like fixing everything. It doesn't mean getting rid of all the parts that are painful to think about. Living in wholeness would mean understanding that this is who you are. You aren't missing any parts. You don't need to be different or better first. You don't have to be fixed, put back together, or reordered to be whole. You are a whole self.

I might need practice to get in touch with all the parts that, put together, make up me. I might have work to do to become more *well*, but not to become more whole. I am whole, and living into my wholeness is a work in progress. I thought I was supposed to have arrived, but *where I am* and *who I am* are two entirely different things.

I know where I am. I am standing here beneath my own judgment and spilled wax, but I am not broken. That is not who I am. Who I am is love. My real self is love. My real self is not an imposter. My real self does not need to arrive. None of that matters. I can be imperfectly, awkwardly real, because I am imperfectly, awkwardly love, which might be the only kind of love we can be.

Being a grown-up is so much simpler if I'm not supposed to have arrived.

The missing piece, the thing keeping me from feeling comfortable in my own skin, wasn't arriving at all. It was *accepting*. The way to feel like a real grown-up is to own who I am, whole, with all my very real flaws and limitations, and with space to become more well. That would be simpler than waiting on myself to change.

I am the way I am for a damn good reason, *and* I am a work in progress. I can accept that. That doesn't make me an imposter. Imposter grown-ups aren't the ones who are still figuring things out—imposter grown-ups are the ones who are pretending to have nothing left to learn.

Being a grown-up is about knowing who you are, your whole self, because you are the way you are for a damn good reason. But it's also about knowing *what* you are. You are a work in progress.

This in-between, unfinished, on-a-journey place—this is

a fine place to be. We don't have to hide until we get it right, and we don't have to get everything right to be worthy of the ground on which we stand. We can breathe all the air we require and take all the time we need. We can take up space. You can't be love in the world if you aren't even taking up space. Where would you love from?

"How are things?" My sister texted me, while I was still working on my jeans situation. I could not adequately explain about the candle wax and the ironing over a text message. But maybe I didn't have to explain anyway. Maybe I could simply take up this spilled-on, messy space.

"Things are okay," I texted back. "Things are good."

CHAPTER 15

Kate at the Coffee Shop

Permission to Try Again

Some people are coffee people, but I come from tea people. Like my mother before me and her mother before her, I grew up on Lipton orange pekoe in the white paper packet. If you were to look in my pantry today, you would find loose-leaf tea and jars of herbs for blending and something called Golden Monkey. You would find caffeinated and decaf and naturally caffeine-free options. You would find black tea. You would find white tea. You would find green tea. There are boxes of tea bags arranged into elaborate towers on more shelves than I think I should admit. I cannot remember to stock breakfast foods, but my tea selection is carefully curated and never runs low, because: priorities.

So when my friend Kate and I decided to meet up for coffee, what I really meant was tea. You can keep your frothy-smooth decoction of coffee beans; I will indulge in the luxury of having someone else pour hot water over a bag of leaves for me and call it good.

"I'll come to you," Kate said, which was very kind of her, given that her house was an hour from mine and neither of us likes to drive. We were meeting up after dinner, because that is when parents sneak out to have conversations without interruptions, and Kate and I have ten kids between us. We have professional-level experience with interruptions. But this time, we were going to have caffeinated beverages *and* conversation on the same night.

I just had to find somewhere for us to meet.

Kate used to live in one of the cool little neighborhoods in downtown San Diego, where there are funky coffee shops on every corner and shops are open all hours of the day. You can get artisanal ice cream scooped at ten o'clock at night if you want to. I've done it.

I live in a beach town outside the city. We have our own laid-back vibe, though not quite the same artisanal ice cream scene. I've lived here since I was a teenager, so you would think I'd know all the good coffee places. Or at least one good coffee place. Or maybe even a mediocre coffee place?

But was I clear enough about my people? MY PEOPLE ARE TEA PEOPLE. We don't know coffee. We can fake it at Starbucks, but that is the extent of our coffee abilities. Did I also mention the pantry, fully stocked and ready to host a high tea? I do not go out for tea. I stay in, and I brew like nobody's business.

But Kate was my pastor as well as my friend, and we were going out for coffee. I mean tea. I just had to find somewhere to buy it.

I wasn't worried at first. Other people drink coffee, even if I do not. The suburbs need to stay caffeinated, so surely, we have suppliers. This is how my reasoning went.

This was a job for the trusty Google. Not a problem. And in fact, my search turned up plenty of options. None sounded *great*—one advertised live "relaxing jazz" performances on-site, another listed "no parking lot" among its assets—but there were several to choose from. As I started scrolling through the list, though, I noticed they all had one thing in common. They all closed by eight p.m.

The one by the beach with the casually chill atmosphere? Closed at eight.

The one that sold coffee and treats from various world-changing nonprofits? Closed at eight.

The one with the supposedly superior coffee that inspires die-hard fans? Closed at eight.

The one with the relaxing jazz? Closed at eight.

(Parents of small children do not need relaxing jazz after dinner, anyway. We will fall asleep sitting up and spill our drinks.)

No way could Kate get to my house before seven, and an hour of driving for an hour of talking followed by an hour of driving home did not seem like an excellent deal.

Fine, I thought. *So much for independent coffee shops. We'll meet at one of the chain shops.* There were four nearby, all in grocery store parking lots. They wouldn't make us feel like fancy coffee consumers, but you know what? We would still have hot drinks. So be it. I mapped them so I could send Kate an address.

Three of *those* would close before nine.

The fourth one closed . . . at nine.

How fast could we talk? That was the question.

I widened my search. I texted people who get up early, because they probably drink coffee. I asked everyone who might have an idea about places to hang out on a school night, and still,

I couldn't find a coffee shop open past nine p.m. anywhere in a twenty-mile radius. Apparently, no one drinks caffeine after curfew out here.

It was Dane who thought to search for coffee counters inside other shops—the grocery store, the bookstore. He was right: the coffee shop inside the bookstore would let us have an indoor table until ten o'clock. So that was where we were, cooling our drinks and pretending not to notice the people rummaging through the bargain bins eighteen inches away.

I could see everything that was wrong with this plan. At no point would either of us think I was interesting for knowing about this place. There would be no joy of discovery, none of the fun that comes with an offbeat little coffee shop. We wouldn't have adventurous new drinks to try, ones with inside-joke names that we didn't really understand and felt ridiculous saying out loud. There wouldn't even be loud music or uncomfortable mood lighting.

I was pretty sure this made me the most boring friend ever: someone who drinks weak tea from a personality-free coffee counter in a strip mall. Not only that—someone who invites you to drive an hour to drink weak tea (or hey, you can have coffee!) from a counter inside a shop in a strip mall. So enticing!

(Of course, if Kate had invited *me* to have tea in a bookstore, I would have had two thoughts. One, *Wow, Kate is clever and resourceful!* And two, *YAY BOOKS.* But this did not occur to me at the time.)

"This is great," Kate said, surveying our surroundings. Neither of us are glass-half-full kind of people, so I raised my eyebrow and cringed, trying to make a face that said, "No, but really, sorry about choosing this place," without having to say it. She didn't roll her eyes or laugh, though. She seemed to be serious.

"This is where you and Dane grew up, right? Did you used to hang out here?"

"Well, yes," I said, and for one second, I would not have been surprised to see our teenage selves coming around the end of the bookshelf. This had been one of our usual places. We couldn't believe they would let us drink our coffee (or tea) while we looked at books we didn't even own. It was like the library on steroids, and you could *buy things*. We have always been at home in bookstores.

"That's so cool," she said again.

She was making small talk, I understood, but she seemed to mean it. The words were inconsequential to her, but they kept turning over in my head. *She sees this differently than I do. She sees ME differently than I do. She sees me how I see everyone else: as perfectly valid human beings, loved and important and worthy of belonging exactly as they are. I wonder whose perspective is most accurate here.*

Was I making this—drinks, friend, talking—harder than it needed to be? Almost surely, because that is what I do. You don't need a certain kind of coffee shop to have connection and conversation. You don't need hipster table settings for human flourishing. I think I knew this.

It's just that it's easier to see the outside things, the ones you can point to and critique and fuss over and maybe change with a few dollars and an accurate GPS app. It's harder to see where you are on the inside.

At church one Sunday, Kate had told us about *eshet chayil*, a Hebrew phrase that means *woman of valor*.[1] Kate found wisdom and beauty in these words that came from another language, another culture, another tradition, and wanted to use them in celebrating all of *us*. Matthew, who usually led us in singing bluesy songs that reminded us of our worth, was going to help. Together they taught us a musical intonation: *"Esh-et chay-il! Woman of valor!"* And we were going to say this, out loud, as a group, to each other. At that moment.

Women began calling out the things they were proud of, the things that made them women of valor. One woman had spoken up in a meeting. One woman had birthed a baby. One woman rode her motorcycle everywhere she wanted to. *"Eshet chayil!"* we chanted. *"Woman of valor!"*[2]

And even as I celebrated those women, even as the words came from my heart and out of my mouth, I began to shrink inside, because I could not think of one thing to say about my own self, not one thing. I was not a woman of valor, and I wanted to hide.

I racked my brain: had I ever done anything worth celebrating? Was there anything about me at all worth mentioning? I didn't have a motorcycle.

Sure, I had birthed a baby—technically, six of them—but not *recently*.

Yes, I had successfully arrived here more or less on time with all of my offspring dressed and fed, which felt like a major accomplishment for us all, but so had everyone else.

I hadn't learned to speak any new languages, hadn't overcome any illnesses, hadn't accomplished anything I could think of or made any new friends. If only I had gotten a promotion! Yes this would have required getting a whole different kind of *job* first, but still. If I could change something on the outside: *Woman of valor!*

Instead, my days were all similar, with nothing much to report. I rolled out of bed today? I didn't get dressed until lunchtime? I forgot to take back the library books? I can't remember the last time I slept through the night? None of these would work.

The point was to see the good in who we were and in what we did every day, I understood that, but I still could not think of anything to say. I couldn't do it then, and I was struggling to do it in the coffee-shop-that-was-a-bookstore. How could I be a woman of valor if I did not have one remarkable thing to report? I still hadn't figured that out, and my life kept confirming it: there was nothing remarkable about me at all. When I looked at my life story, I saw small, boring, quiet, overlookable. Why hadn't I ever lived in a city with twenty-four-hour takeout? Why hadn't I collected adventures that involved salsa dancing and chocolate croissants? Why hadn't I lived a more exciting story than this one?

Well, because those weren't my stories to live. This was my story. And Kate, sitting across the table from me, was asking about my story as though she was really interested, as though it didn't matter that mine was a quiet story, as though quieter stories weren't less important just because they didn't have an exotic backdrop. Nothing stays exotic forever, anyway. Eventually even croissants at two a.m. can become familiar. My own story isn't fancy, but it's mine, and it's real.

I thought about that while we waited for our drinks to cool.

This—sitting with Kate at a slightly sticky bistro table on a Tuesday night, talking about our families and our histories and how on earth we ever get anything done—was the real me. (It was the real Kate, too.) This fit in my real story. Not quite as well as staying home for tea, but close. This was me. Another version might have been more fun, more surprising, more intriguing, or at least more shimmery, but if I don't show up—the real me, the possibly uninteresting me, the me who does not know how to find a coffee shop—love doesn't get to show up where I would have been. There's just a placeholder instead of love. A place-holder isn't the real thing. You can't be love if you won't show up.

Showing up, I decided, when I was finally able to sip my mint tea without scalding the roof of my mouth, was the point. Showing up, real and without glitter to distract from who and what you are, is brave.

Showing up in my life as myself: *woman of valor*. Trying again when I realize I'm hiding again, and when I discover new patterns to change, new layers to uncover: *woman of valor*. Knowing myself and trusting myself: *woman of valor*. Giving the people around me space to be who *they* are in their actual lives, too, no special accomplishments necessary: *woman of valor*. This is me, and this is where I am. *Woman of valor*.

I have a real life and a real history. Not an ideal life. Not a cool life. A real one.

Being who I am—uncool, in sneakers and a ponytail, with dark circles that have lived under my eyes since my oldest child was a baby—will always be simpler than trying to be better, or fancier, or more interesting. Real-and-falling-apart is always better than fake-but-put-together.

Real and falling apart is where love will meet us. Showing up there to wait: *woman of valor*.

CHAPTER 16

Try Saying the True Things

Permission to Choose Vulnerability

Sometimes truth needs help to find its way into the light.

My friend Jessica is the kind of person who looks you in the eye, so you know you are seen, even if you're just saying hello. She asks good questions, waits for the answers, and does not fill in the silence if you take a while. It's like she wants to hear what you have to say. She kept asking me a very simple question, one that did not require a lot of research or background knowledge. I kept not answering, because I did not know the answer.

"Are you coming?" she asked.

She was starting a women's group in my neighborhood, and I was a woman, so this seemed like a good fit.

"We're meeting at Bonnie's house," she said. "You know Bonnie."

I did not.

"You do! You must. Dave and Bonnie? *That* Bonnie?"

Still no.

"You do! You'll know her when you see her."

I would not.

But that wasn't really what worried me. I just wasn't sure what a women's group would *be*. A book club without the books, maybe? I didn't know.

I do know what a group of people is like, though. You put on your ethically made statement earrings and your casually fabulous hair, you bring a cheese tray with a selection of gluten-free crackers, and because you're getting together in a group on a weeknight, all you can talk about is how busy you are.

How are you? "I'm fine! Busy, but fine!"

How's work? "Busy. So busy."

How's that whole being-a-parent thing? "Good. Busy. Kids never stop moving, have you noticed this? So much to do, so busy."

How's the state of your soul? "Wait, what?"

See, that one doesn't fit. You have to stick to questions that can be answered with "busy."

It sounded exhausting.

Why would I show up for that? Why would anyone? But we all want to be seen and known, we all want to feel safe and held, and we're mostly not opposed to the idea of having a regular rhythm of turning toward each other again and again, maybe around a plate of hummus and veggies.

It's just that it's also terrifying. What if we can't relate? What if no one is anything like us? What if we look around the room, and everyone is more put-together, more beautiful, more recently bathed, more unafraid, more successful at being a person? What if we're the worst? What if the conversation is all about freezer cooking and anniversary sales, which I know nothing about? The getting-ready part of the evening feels safer than the showing-up part. But if I spend all my getting-ready time making my outside say, *I am trying to make you comfortable with my existence, starting with my appearance*, it's hard to open up and show people the real inside story, the story that starts with being fully yourself. And if I put all my energy into the prep work beforehand, I'll be spent before I ever get to the human connection part of the evening. Do I focus on being liked, or do I aim for being known?

I want to feel safe *with* other people, but I also want to be safe *from* those same other people. I don't think I'm alone in this. That's why we hide behind our clever graphic tees. We share nothing, or we dwell in drama (and preferably drama about someone who's not in the room). We clear kitchen counters and light candles and bring finger foods. We apply fresh lipstick before we walk in the door. We want to be known, but we don't want to actually let ourselves be seen. We're drawn to the *idea* of community but can't quite put down the masks that separate us from the real thing. It's a complicated dance of push-pull, hope-fear, want-need. We believe in our own separateness so much that we're afraid to show up in the ways that are necessary for real connection. That's what it's like to hang out with a new group of people.

But I do love Jess, and it wasn't far to drive, and I was free on Thursday nights. And I would not object to having more friends. I'm not good at being around other people—I don't even know how to assemble a proper cheese tray—but I am not *against* the idea.

"I'll be there," I texted Jessica. Texting is easier than committing out loud.

Bonnie's front door was open by the time I parked my car at her curb, but I still knocked and waited for someone to let me in. You never know when you have the address wrong, or the time wrong, or the wrong day on the calendar. (I say this only because I regularly show up at the wrong time. Invite me to your house at your own peril.) If I'm showing up on the wrong day, the least I can do is not walk into a stranger's kitchen without knocking first.

But I wasn't wrong. It was the right day. There were women in Bonnie's living room, holding glasses of lemon water and looking varying degrees of uncomfortable. *Why did these women show up?* I wondered. *What do they want?* Presumably, they wanted to be seen, to be known, and to not have to wear those suede booties with the heels anymore if they didn't feel like it. One woman kicked hers off over by the couch.

Bonnie (whom I really did not know) passed out index cards, and Jessica told us each to write down, privately, what we wanted out of this group. Then we all set our cards out in Bonnie's kitchen and living room and on the dining room table, and we walked here and there, reading each other's anonymous hopes. And here our separateness started to melt away, as we read our own thoughts in other people's handwriting. What did we want? A place to be vulnerable, everyone agreed. A place where saying real, true things was normal and expected. Brené Brown would be our patron saint. (Unless patron saints have to be actually dead and sainted? If that's what patron saints are, then never mind; Brené can be our very alive inspiration.)

Jess took us at our word, and started leading our meetings with questions like, *What are you angry with God about?* and *Where are you hurt?* Jess does not mess around. "Bring a journal!" she would say. And then Bonnie would offer backup paper and pens, so you couldn't even skip the hard questions by pretending you'd forgotten your journal. We would write about our anger, our hurt, our experiences, our hopes, our ideas, and our fears, and then we would say them out loud if we wanted to, too. If we ended the evening worn out—and sometimes we did—it wasn't because we were treading water and bobbing around on the surfaces of our own personal seas. It was because we'd gone deep with ourselves and with each other.

I didn't even know I needed to get to know myself. I thought I knew myself because I was clear on all my faults, but those are just surface-level. There's no depth to a list like that. There's no understanding about what you want or who you could become. There's no compassion for where you've been and what you've been through. There's no insight into what makes your heart beat and your breath catch in your throat. How well can anyone else know you if you don't even know yourself?

After we looked into our own hearts, we would hold up what we saw to each other. *Do you see what I see here? Can anyone relate? Do you see me?*

"I'm having a high-anxiety week," I told the women one Thursday night. I felt my heart racing as I spoke, because who knew *what* they would say. Would they decide I was too needy, too difficult, too high maintenance? Would they insist, so helpfully, that my problems were spiritual failings? Would they tell me what they thought I should do, and how easy my problems would be to solve? That never helps. Would they stop seeing my whole self, and start seeing me as A Person with Anxiety?

You don't have to be fully vulnerable with everyone in your life, but trust is built one story at a time, and after a thousand shared stories, I thought Bonnie and Jess and the others could handle this one. So I took a deep breath and kept talking. I told them how Dane had been away all week, and how my brain thinks its job is to stay vigilant in order to keep everyone alive while he's gone. I told them how every decision seemed enormous, how making a wrong choice seemed both inevitable and unforgivable, as though I was always seconds away from tumbling into the mouth of a volcano. I told them how it felt like I couldn't breathe, as though my chest had been wrapped up too tightly, like I was wearing the world's worst turtleneck. I told them what I knew—that the anxiety was only trying to protect me, and if it's trying to protect me, but that it wasn't my best, truest self talking. I knew that. And still, the anxiety was just so loud and hard to reason with. I told them everything, and then I waited to see what they would do with my words.

"That *sucks*," they said.

"I've been there," one voice said.

Another said, "I understand."

"What helps?" they asked. "What have you tried? What needs to change?"

There was no uncomfortable silence. No avoiding eye contact. No quick reduction, no changing their understanding of me from a whole human being to just a sliver of one. They did not try to fix me, though they offered to help. They did not foist cheap, easy answers into my lap, as though my pain might spread to them if they didn't contain it quickly enough. They did not call me broken. They called me seen. Heard. Known. This is how they were love for me—they let me bring my scary thing out into the light until it wasn't so scary any more. Love shows up in truth—and you can't tell the truth while you're pretending to be who you think you're supposed to be. You can't get at the truth without being vulnerable. We practiced making space for truth, and truth makes space for love.

The hard part of our gatherings was not in the tidying up and the finding clean jeans to throw on at the end of a long day. The hard work was in showing up and being seen for who we were.

One night after our time together, I picked up Glennon Doyle's book, *Love Warrior*, and read this: "a woman who has recovered her true identity as a Love Warrior is the most powerful force on earth."[1] Glennon says a Love Warrior knows her light is stronger than the darkness. A Love Warrior knows who she is and what she is here to do. That is what we were doing at Bonnie's house; we were becoming Love Warriors. We were learning together that we are love, we are here to be love in the world, and the best place to practice being love is in the presence of vulnerability.

And in the sacred space that vulnerability creates, we practiced showing up as love for each other—not by correcting, or judging, or shutting each other down. Love does not look like that. Love looks like making room on the couch and pouring another cup of tea. Love looks like honoring other perspectives, because people are the way they are for a damn good reason, and because love is willing to learn. Love looks like staying open to truth, even if the truth looks like pain or anger or doubt or a general readiness to burn it all down and start over.

When I did that—when I stayed open to telling the truth and holding the truth—I grew closer to Bonnie and Jess and all the other women in the room. I grew closer to me, too, because I could see myself more clearly.

We even grew closer to God, because God is love, and God

is truth. God is with us in our vulnerability. God is not afraid of the truth of our lives. Even when that truth looks like crying and raging and insisting, *I don't understand this. I am angry about that. Why does it work this way? What is up with this whole freaking WORLD?*

God is not surprised. God is already aware of the things that piss us off and the things that break our hearts and the things that leave us flattened in the middle of the night, even if we've been afraid to say them out loud.

Saying things out loud is part of the deal. I was afraid vulnerability would drive everyone away, but instead, it drew us together. Preparing a smoother, busier version of myself would have been so much easier, but then my outside would have been all shiny while my inside self twisted and hid. The inside and outside wouldn't have matched up. If you want things to feel simpler, being your whole, true—and truly vulnerable—self is the way. Bringing your real, inside self out is the only way. You can't be love if you won't be real.

I want the love. I want the truth. God is in both, and that's where I want to be. And the way in is vulnerability.

CHAPTER 17

The Wisdom of the Crowd

Permission to Find Your Voice

I have never wanted a tattoo. I've never been drawn to the idea at all, not for one minute. I'm not sure why. I'm not opposed to tattoos on other people; I've just never wanted one for myself.

Okay, yes, I guess the process itself freaks me out. The idea of holding still while someone uses a needle-apparatus to apply ink under my skin doesn't sound super appealing. The needles are a little bit of a turnoff. And no, "being decisive" does not rank among my strengths. How would I ever settle on what tattoo to get? That might also be part of it. But I think it's mostly the *permanence* factor that concerns me. I understand that you can choose something beautiful to be reminded of forever—but is there anything I really want to be reminded of *forever*? "Personal style" and "it seemed like a good idea at the time" overlap more often than I would like, maybe too often for me to feel good about making a permanent style decision.

I want space to change my mind. And have we forgotten the needle-apparatus situation?

This has never added up to something which interests me on even the tiniest level. I don't have any philosophical objections. I don't have any deep-seated anxieties or fears or negative experiences to overcome. It's just not my thing. Tea is my thing. Owning more necklaces than clothes is my thing. Tattoos, not so much my thing.

So it's possible I should have known the answer immediately when Dane came home one day and asked if I thought maybe we should get tattoos.

"What do you think?" he asked. Three of our friends—separately! in unrelated instances!—had all gone under the needle that week and were rocking new body art. Dane and I sat together on the couch and scrolled through their in-process and reveal photos: one friend at a counter waiting to be called back; another in a chair, smiling at the camera while the tattoo artist was at work; another peeling back a bandage to reveal red skin and new ink. It did seem as though, suddenly, everyone around us was getting tattooed. Maybe it was time.

I'd never wanted to before, but what if I'd just never *let* myself want to? What if I was listening for what I thought I was *supposed* to do, instead of listening for my own inner voice? Because, honestly, there are a lot of voices that would like my attention. There is my true voice: the still, small one inside me, the one that tells me the truth and points me toward love and forward momentum (or at least toward the next right thing). That voice sometimes tells me what to do.

But it's not like that's the only voice offering up its opinion on the matter. There's the voice of fear, of course, but there's also the voice of the world around me. There's the voice of my neighbor and the voices of my friends and the voice of my new favorite book. There's the voice of advertising, letting me know what's wrong with me and what I should buy to fix it. There's the voice of cultural norms, telling me what people usually do, telling me what's allowed. All those voices have opinions about how I should live my life. And if I'm not paying attention, if I'm not listening closely, I might not notice that those voices aren't even my own.

What if I'd been doing what was expected instead of thinking about what I really wanted? Whose voice had I been listening to? Mine or not-mine? Maybe the thing that was expected of me was the thing I actually wanted. Maybe the outside voice and the inside voice were the same on this one. Maybe they overlapped. Or maybe I'd listened so well to the outside voices that I didn't recognize them as foreign anymore.

I thought of the elegant calligraphy and simple designs I'd admired on other people's arms and shoulders and ankles. I knew two different couples with matching typography tattoos, each one showing off initials that appeared to have been printed right on their skin. Several friends had handwriting recorded in their flesh—a mother's, a sister's, an artist's—reminding them of a sacred phrase every time they caught a glimpse of their own wrist or forearm. I've seen sleek, modern shapes: hearts, stars, a safety pin. One friend has a drawing sketched by another friend on her arm. One friend has a mandala-like circle, an invitation to meditation on her own body. My sister has a symbol she designed herself on one shoulder; another girlfriend sports "9 3/4," and gets to be reminded every day that reality is not always what it seems.

It's like our friends were declaring a vision of themselves

and putting it down in ink. In elementary school, I hated putting things in ink. Your mistakes would last forever, every little slanted "H" or backwards "R" mocking you from the page and making you feel cranky every time you glanced at your otherwise-amazing drawing of a marching band. But my friends didn't seem concerned. They were willing to put their sense of self on permanent display.

Who would I be with ink on my wrist? Would I be more defined? More settled? Maybe a tattoo would make me cooler. It would at least make me more decisive, because I would have to choose something.

"I don't know," Dane said. "Would you want to?"

I'd never wanted this, had I? Or *had* I? What if I really was the worst at listening to my own voice?

"How do you know what you want?" I asked Dane. "You know, *in life*."

He loves questions like this, where I pin him in a corner of the kitchen and basically dare him to change the subject while I open up existential crises. (He does not.) It's a thing we do for fun. (Not really.)

"Um," he said. "Hmm."

"Right?" I asked.

"Do you mean how does one know what one wants in general? Or how do I personally know what I want?"

"Either. Both."

"Hmm. Well."

That's about what I thought, too.

How do you tell the difference between the voice of the world and the voice of yourself? Both have things to say. Both can repeat themselves on a loop in your head without your permission. Both can keep you up at night. And both can sound right, when you hear them and speak them. Both voices can sound right.

But . . . I think they *feel* different.

The voice that tells me what's normal, what's expected, what I should do and who I should be—that voice feels safe. I know I won't be questioned if I go along with it. It feels solid, the kind of solid I can hide behind—because it's the voice of the crowd, and you can always hide behind a crowd. This voice might feel like it has its permission slip signed, but it is not my own. This voice might tell me not to get a tattoo, or it might tell me I should, but either way, my best decisions never come from listening to this one.

My own voice—the one that may not give me the whole plan but does whisper the next right thing—doesn't always feel safe, but it feels true. This voice feels solid too, but it's a different kind of solid. This kind of solidity doesn't give me anything to hide behind. It gives me one solid step forward, even if I can't see the one after that, even if I don't know where I'm going or where I'll end up. (It hadn't given me a solid step toward a tattoo yet, but maybe it was going to?) The voice that rises up from my true self feels different than all the other voices. It feels like me.

I can hear the difference between my voice and the world's, too, if I'm listening for it. I can hear the difference when I ask myself what I want, and I listen to see whose voice pipes up inside my own head. Is it a friend's voice, or Dane's, or some long-ago teacher's? Or does this voice sound like me? That's another way to tell.

I might be freaked out by what either voice says—the voice that is mine or the one that comes from outside—but even the fear is a clue. If I'm afraid of stepping into the unknown, that is one sort of clue, because doing what's expected isn't unknown. That's what makes it expected. If I'm afraid of what people will think, that's a different sort of clue, because no one will question me if I stick to the script. Feeling those fears might mean I'm hearing my own voice—but following those fears would be listening to something outside myself.

If you're going to hear your own voice and recognize it all the time, you have to practice listening for it, and you have a million chances every single day. What will you eat for breakfast? When do you need to recharge? Do you want to meet up for coffee, or stay home and go to bed early? You practice listening around the breakfast table and in the pillow aisle at IKEA, so you know the sound of yourself when it comes to tattoos. I know this and have been trying to practice.

But it's easy to let the habit of listening in the little things slip away, because the stakes feel so low. It doesn't feel worth upsetting anyone over small things. *Sure, we can have that for dinner. Yes, I will show up. Okay, I can stay up another hour to get this done. No, I don't need to make time for my own ideas right now. I can wait for some other day.*

The problem with not listening in the little things is that by the time the big things come along, my voice is buried so deep I can barely remember what it sounds like. Trying to decide on anything becomes an anxious weighing of pros and cons and best practices and objective advice and outside opinions. It's a tangle of wants and needs and expectations, when it could be as simple as asking: *What do you really want?*

So did I want a tattoo? Did I not want a tattoo? Maybe I wanted a nose ring; I don't know.

Making things simpler starts with sorting out the voices, so you can decide which one you're going to listen to. If my true self—confused as it may be sometimes—is love, if I am the way I am for a good reason, then I have a voice that is worth listening to. My own voice is pointing me toward love, but also toward truth, because love and truth are buddies. They go together.

Making things simpler looks like knowing the sound of your own voice, and knowing you always have permission to do what you need to do. It's not asking around for opinions. It's not crowdsourcing your truth. True simplicity would be knowing that you can trust yourself to do the next right thing, whatever that turns out to be.

But seriously, am I going to get the tattoo?

I was not afraid of what people would think. My family would not care; they're cool with tattoos. My friends would not care; half my friends have them already. My work would not be affected; I work in my house and communicate with the world using words on a screen. The people I see most often are my kids, who are in no way invested in my style choices. I did not belong to any communities that would be even momentarily surprised. That is what I am saying here.

I was not excited about needles, but the actual experience would end, and anyway, I'd been practicing some yoga breathing that could help.

I could imagine tattoos that I really, really liked.

So why not get one? Why not?

But then I heard it. Small, quiet, from my gut: *A tattoo would feel like covering myself, and my self does not want to be covered.* For most people, a tattoo is an expression of self. An expression is not a covering; an expression is a *revealing*. But to me, that was how it felt. A tattoo would feel like covering up the self I had been given. It would feel like another something to hide behind.

And then I heard this: *A tattoo would feel like being pinned to this moment, and I want room to grow.* I want room to become more of who I really am. I want to keep shedding the outside layers that don't fit anymore, and a tattoo would be a layer I could not remove. I would outgrow whatever I chose, and then it would become an exercise in compassion and love for my former self— both of which are good things but are not what I want to use my skin for at this time.

And besides, of all the beauty I had seen on other people's bodies, none of it called to me. When I imagined gorgeous designs, I never imagined them on me. When I tried, it felt all wrong, like wearing someone else's shoes.

That was why not. A tattoo might make me more interesting. It might be an exercise in self-determination. It might be a declaration of some sort of self-awareness. But it would not be me. I listened, and that is what I heard.

"I don't want one," I told Dane.

"I don't think I do, either," he said. "I was just asking."

CHAPTER 18

Do This First

Permission to Draw a Finish Line

I love my bed. This could be explained by the whole "absence makes the heart grow fonder" phenomenon, by which I mean I do not get to spend nearly as much time lying down as I would like. But even so, it would take a *lot* of together time for me to want a break from hanging out with my BFF (also known as "the pillow").

Some nights, though, you would not guess that this is true, based on the amount of tossing and turning and fluffing of pillows—okay, *smashing* of pillows—and heaving of sighs that goes on in the night. My desire to *be* asleep does not always translate into the ability to *get* to sleep.

For a long time, I was not really relaxing peacefully into bed so much as I was falling face-first into the sheets when I ran out of steam and could not do one more thing.

Even then, I would lie awake and stare at the sheets. Yes, I would have preferred to be asleep and therefore unaware of the presence of sheets. No, that did not seem to be an option.

I should have been tired. I had barely stopped moving for eighteen hours straight. I could just think of so many good things to do with those hours, is all, and there was never enough time in the day. Bedtime did not arrive when I had finished all the things and was ready to sleep; bedtime arrived when I gave up. I still had tasks unfinished. And not even exciting tasks like, *I haven't finished carving my masterpiece to rival the Venus de Milo.* Just tasks like, *there are still dinner dishes in the sink, no one will have clean underwear in the morning because the laundry is still wet in the washing machine but the towels in the dryer need folding before they can be moved, I haven't sent the two emails that sit half-composed in my inbox or replied to anyone's text messages all afternoon, the grocery list for the morning's errands does not yet exist, and I am pretty sure I need to pay the library fines before we can stop there to check out more books.*

This was my routine: keep doing things until I could not do one more thing, and then fall into bed. My body kept seeming less and less excited about this plan, refusing to fall asleep and generally feeling discontented as I lay there in what should have been the happiest place on earth, my favorite place, my bed. At the end of every day, no matter whether I'd paid attention to the things that make me come alive, no matter whether I'd rested, no matter how I'd prioritized, no matter how many expectations I'd ignored, no matter how Dane and I divided up the tasks that could be shared, there were always projects unfinished, emails unanswered, and chores left undone. I hadn't done it all, so I felt like I hadn't done enough.

I lay there in bed, my brain cataloguing all the things that weren't yet finished and making new lists of things that would need to be done tomorrow. Every night. Every tomorrow.

And then, I knew that when I did wake up, the new day would not be a blank slate. Yesterday would bleed through into tomorrow, so every day would start out a little bit too full before my feet even hit the floor. That was something else to lie awake thinking about at two o'clock in the morning: how my life had become an actual hamster wheel, just going and going and never stopping. When I was little, we went to a park that had kid-sized wheels to climb into. We would clamber in, two or three of us at a time, and run and run and get nowhere, and this was somehow considered entertainment. There was no stopping place in that game, but when we were tired, we would tumble out and collapse, wobbly-legged, onto that foam padding that covers the dirt at playgrounds.

But your life, I think, is not supposed to be a hamster wheel, always going around and around without stops or even mile markers. This is what I would tell myself at two-thirty, but by two forty-five I was back to making my list of things to do so I would not forget it in the morning. This is how you let dishes keep you from ever resting.

I was pretty sure that insomnia meant my body was trying to tell me something. I couldn't always hear things during the day because my life was noisy, so I figured my body had to talk to me at night. This is a strategy many of my children have tried. Toddlers, in particular, seem to believe that nighttime is an excellent time to tell me things. Maybe my body and I were in a toddler stage of communication. One of us was learning to talk, and the other one was trying to decipher sounds that might be messages or might just be random confused noises.

I am trying to learn to pay attention to whatever my body wants me to know. I want to practice making changes before my heart itself cracks open. I don't want to wait until I'm broken-down and depleted to notice that something is wrong and ask myself what it might be. So lying in bed, instead of just being flattened by the feelings, I decided to try looking right at them. I stared at my frustration about all the things I'd left incomplete. I stared at the way I felt unsettled. I stared at the way I ended each day unsatisfied, and I looked at how there was no closure. I saw how everything stayed open, all the time.

You know what happens when you leave your doors open all the time? You get flies. You get mosquitoes, and the occasional wild bird, and in this weather, lizards. Once, when I left the front door open, the neighbor's cat walked in.

If you leave the fridge open, you waste a whole lot of energy and every good thing goes bad. If you leave the bread open, the stuff you depend on for nourishment will be stale before you take one bite. Some things need closing.

If those things stay closed, they don't do any good. They can't fulfill their purpose, not at all. But if they stay open, they aren't any good to anyone, either. I had to close some things so there would be a point to opening them up again.

I once read that saying "DONE" as you finish a task makes you feel more satisfied and settled, because you're putting that work behind you. DONE! But I am never DONE. I don't even know what that would look like. There are always more dishes to wash and projects to start and laundry to run and messages to answer and ideas to consider before I've come close to finishing the ones I'm working on. Even if you're not letting the voice of fear dictate your schedule, even if you refuse to be busy, even if you've given yourself permission to say no, even if you don't do all the things that the Grown-Up Responsibility Checklist says you should, there are still too many things.

And if you happen to live with—or *know*—any other people, they all bring their own agendas into your life, disrupting your best intentions for sticking to your plan and getting things done. (By "agendas," I mean little things like "their need to reschedule your appointment, the fact that they've lost their pen, their wondering whether you're done with that muffin, their indiscriminate use of 'reply all,' which blows up your inbox for the rest of the morning, and/or their musings on the meaning of life." That's all.) Your sense of order—or even balance—is shaky at best.

These truths keep coming back to wrestle with me, because I am forgetful and tend to fall into old patterns, even if I know there's a better way. Comfortable patterns serve us, like pajamas. They're soft and predictable; they just don't prepare us to face the world. And anyway, there's always more to learn. Life keeps circling around and around, bringing us the same lessons again and again, but showing them to us from another angle.

So maybe it was no wonder that I was awake at three a.m. Maybe my insomnia had its own damn good reason for showing up.

Maybe its reason was that my current method of getting through the day was stupid. I was switching between tasks, piling things to do on top of other things to do, and never getting to the most important stuff. I wasn't marking my beginnings and endings, and my days were all running together like melting ice cream. Every day was incomplete. There was no finish line to cross, so I just kept racing. I never had enough time.

Somewhere in my head, I was aware that my worth and my to-do list were not related, but the never-done-ness still felt awful. And my brain couldn't shut itself off. I was just powering down the machine of my body, not recharging at the source and restarting in the morning.

Punching your pillow always seems like it will be more helpful than it turns out to be at times like this.

The day was over. Had I done enough? I had not. I could never do enough, and it's only a short leap from "I never do enough" to "I'm not enough." Not good enough, not focused enough, not smart enough to figure this out. There just wasn't enough time. There would never be enough time.

That was what I heard when I started listening to myself. *There would never be enough time.* Why couldn't I make it all work? Why couldn't I finish all the things?

Well, maybe because I'm human, and I have limitations, and I am that way for a damn good reason.

I couldn't change the *being human* part of myself. I couldn't change the *having human limitations* part, either. But *something* had to change. There was never enough time to do all the things. And the number of things to do would not really change. Everyone needed to eat every day and also have clean socks with alarming regularity. Projects needed to be tended to, or else they weren't projects; they were just ideas that would float away. And everyone needed love and attention. Even me. So those things couldn't go. And the amount of time in a day was unlikely to increase a whole lot, according to physics. At three-thirty, it occurred to me that there was only one thing I *could* change. I could change how I would define ENOUGH.

My yoga instructor, who is actually a video on my phone, sometimes says that just showing up on the mat is a victory. It doesn't matter if you can contort your body into octopus-like shapes; it doesn't matter if all you do is breathe. If you show up on that mat, you have already won. That is enough. Everything else is a bonus.

I had been living my life as though victory was the perfect headstand. I was pretending that "enough" meant "everything." That's just a bad definition. The dictionary would never have agreed to that. This is what my body was trying to tell me. I had to redefine the whole thing. I had to figure out what my own just-enough victory would be.

The next morning, I went straight to my emergency blank notebook stash, which I keep better stocked than our first aid kit. We don't even have a first aid kit; we have a box of Band-Aids and some arnica cream. But I have a stack of notebooks in three different sizes, with blank and lined pages of varying paper textures, because when I hear "Be Prepared," I think: *notebooks*.

I picked out a mini Moleskine with just enough room to write down maybe three things per page. I had tried lots of times before to make long, thorough lists of all the tasks I thought I needed to do in a day—but at the end of the day, it just left me with a really detailed record of everything that hadn't been done. This notebook was going to be different. This was going to be my Enough List.

I had been imagining my life as one of the big sketchbooks in my stack, all blank pages with lots of space to fill and fill and fill. But I'm really more like the tiny lined Moleskine, and my days are the pages. I can only fit so many things on a page, and I don't know how many pages there will be, so there's no sense in letting one spill over onto all the others. Sometimes you write down your few things and you still have space to doodle around the edges. Other pages have their list laid out plain and will not fit one thing more. But either way, there is a limit to what goes in. I had to make the limits clear to my Planning Self so that my Carrying-Out-the-Plan Self would not keel over and die before we got halfway through the book.

I will choose three things, I thought. *That will be enough. Three things, and if I get to them, I will have accomplished enough for today.* This sounded like such a reasonable plan. I approved.

Then I wrote down seventeen things, all crammed in tiny print between the lines, because I could not go from infinity to three in one try.

Luckily, "enough" is not something you have to pin down in one hour on a Wednesday morning. I can keep redefining what matters and what's enough every day until forever, and I probably will.

I finished four of the seventeen things that day, and I told myself this was a successful experiment. My list was a work in progress, just like me.

I did not move the other thirteen things to the next page. I crossed them all out instead, and told myself to start over by thinking of what would be enough for tomorrow. What was most important to me? I didn't need to list out the urgent stuff—urgency sorts itself out. That stuff gets done whether it's on the list or not. I figured this out quickly. My list needed to be made up of something else. This was not a list of what I HAD to do each day; this was a list of what I would feel best about having done. This was a list of what mattered most. It was a list of what I would be proud of doing. That's what went into the notebook.

One day the list said: *Send the email. Talk to Dane about the thing. Take the kids to the pool.* Another day it was: *Figure out what we're eating this week. Read over the draft. Call to reschedule.* Did other things happen, too? For sure. Did I care if they didn't? Not so much. Because I had decided what was enough, and clean sinks weren't on the list. Neither was inbox zero.

Instead of ending each day feeling like I'd fallen behind, I had a built-in sense of accomplishment in the evenings. *I finished my three things! I did what mattered most!*

There was enough time, and I did enough.

And if I didn't finish all three things, I got to practice giving myself grace. Some days are messy. Some days nothing goes according to plan. That's just life. It doesn't mean I'm disorganized or lazy or behind; it means I'm living. On those days, I get to practice letting go and being okay. I can begin again in the morning. Learning how to live as a self with limits is simpler than pretending you have none.

Making the list is a tiny practice in naming the truth—the truth that I am okay, even if I can't do it all. Today is enough, whatever it holds, even if some things are left for tomorrow. Love says, *you were always enough.* This was my invitation to practice believing it.

CHAPTER 19

I Have Other Gifts

Permission for Celebration

At Bonnie's house, we were planning the calendar for our women's group. What were we going to read or discuss or do together, and when? We all had some vague ideas, but nothing was coming together. A little ball of angst started rolling around in my belly, because I like when things *do* come together, and also, what if someone handed the calendar to me? These days I like calendars best when they're just decorative. I would rather wait until the last minute to see how things are going instead of making plans months in advance. No one else seemed really eager to jump in and start filling up the dates either, though, so I was feeling a little bit concerned for us all.

Jessica, our fearless leader, took my anxious presence as a sign that maybe I was trying to communicate something to her. "Do you want to help with the planning?" she asked.

"Me?" I bounced in my seat like a skittish rabbit. "Oh, no.

Nope. Not me. No thank you. I'm not the best with calendars. At all."

Then Jessica did the thing she does when she finds herself outside of her own zone of genius: she waved her hand in front of her face like it was no big deal, like she was waving away a wisp of smoke, like she was clearing the air. "You have other gifts," she said.

I have other gifts. This is what Jessica says when she isn't willing to pretend to measure up, and she means it, too. This thing in front of her may not be her jam, but oh well. She has other gifts.

My chest always relaxes a little when she says that, because of course, she is right. Of course, you don't need to be gifted at all the things. Of course, it would be silly to expect yourself to do it all. Of course.

And Jess does have other gifts—gifts like wisdom and insight, and compassion and openness, and creating safe spaces where people can be vulnerable, and also making music that fills up your soul using nothing but her own vocal cords.

If you know what your gifts are, it's not so scary to have some faults. This is an idea I like a lot. Do I have any gifts, though? If I do, it's hard to see them around my enormous list of *meh*. I have no phone skills, I have no ability to go with the flow, I cannot meet new people without being weird and awkward, and I have never yet learned to go to bed at a reasonable hour.

Worse, I spend a whole lot of time listening to fear. (I might know not to *follow* it, but I can still hear it talking.) Fear tells me all kinds of things. Fear tells me that everyone I love might stop liking me. Fear tells me I won't be able to fix things or change things or make things right. Fear tells me to avoid pain at all costs—and that I'd really better help everyone else avoid theirs, too. Fear tells me about a whole list of bad things that might come to pass, and also about the vague cloud of unfortunate possibilities. I hear everything fear has to say. I don't usually do what it tells me, but I'm still thinking about it and arguing with it and creating contingency plans for getting around it *all the time.*

I'm not much better with shame, either—it visits like a door-to-door salesperson who rings the bell and then won't stop talking long enough for you to say *no, thank you* and shut the door. It doesn't even take that long for me to start buying what shame is selling—that I'm not good enough, that I've probably overlooked something important, that things would be better for everyone if I would just make myself smaller and that, honestly, I really should have learned to blow-dry my hair by now. I hear the voice of shame, and then I walk around trying to avoid shame triggers (which would basically consist of all human interaction, as well as alone time with my thoughts). This is not one of my strong points.

Yes, I have learned the truth about fear and shame before, but I forget the things I know, and I have to learn them over and over and over again. Maya Angelou taught us that when you know better, you do better—and still, sometimes I forget all the better I know.[1]

If I have any gifts, it's hard to see them past all *that.* But while sitting around the coffee table with Bonnie and Jess and the other women in the room, I have also learned this: knowing all the things that are wrong with me is not really knowing myself. That's only seeing half of me. If I want to be myself, I have to know myself, and that means knowing all the things, not just knowing my fear, or my shame, or what I *should* be good at. So who am I?

I am not the person who should plan the calendar, but I am another kind of person: I am a person who is willing. I am willing to hold on. I am willing to do hard things. I am willing to find a better way. I am willing to see problems and to listen for what needs to change. I am willing to pay attention and to learn first without jumping in to fix things I don't understand. I am a person who is willing to be wrong and to try again, and to say all the things and invite everyone else to say all their things, too. I am a person who holds tight to the belief that solutions are possible, that taking sides will get us nowhere, and that there is always another way to see things, no matter what the issue. I have faith that there's a better way, and that we can move toward it. Those sound kind of like gifts, I guess.

What else? Well, I am a person who believes in our own connection to one another—I believe deeply that we are all the same, that we are made of the same stuff and have the same capacity for love and the same need for belonging—and I believe that understanding and acting on that oneness will open up a little piece of heaven on earth. That belief is a gift. It makes my life better, at the very least.

What else do I know about myself? I am a person who meets needs (including my own) before wants (including everyone else's). I can be good at togetherness—or at least good at sitting on Bonnie's couch—once I get over the awkwardness of getting to know someone. I am practicing walking in the wilderness, if that's what I have to do to live a life I believe in. I'm learning to be okay with other people thinking I'm wrong as long as I'm being myself.

And even though I'm a person who has spent days, weeks, and even years acutely aware of every message fear and shame have to offer, I don't believe in them. I believe in love. I believe in acting from a place of love, not a place of fear. I believe in listening to my spirit, and if the thing trying to drive me is fear, I believe in waiting to do anything until I can hear what love has to say. This is all true about me. These things could be gifts.

So what if all the clean clothes in my house live in laundry baskets? So what if I haven't replied to all the emails? So what if I have to set actual reminders on my phone to tell me to go outside and get some fresh air once in a while? So what if I cannot work a calendar, and get cranky in the afternoon, and have not solved any global crises single-handedly? Okay, well. I have other gifts.

The bad things do not cancel out the good things. Believing that is simpler than expecting to have every gift. I can do some things, and I can't do others that I wish I could. This maybe should not be shocking, given that everyone has a mix of good things and not-so-good things on the inside.

And anyway, maybe knowing your faults *is* a gift. When we're in touch with our own flaws *and* our own privilege *and* our own goodness *and* our own confusion *and* our own mistakes—all of our good things and all of the not-so-good—we can relate to everyone else in theirs. It's harder to imagine someone else is all-terrible if we know what's less than impressive about ourselves. That's part of what "loving your enemies" means. It means not dividing the world up into good and bad, worthy and unworthy, even though the dividing feels so satisfying.

Owning your gifts is another way of saying, *This is me. I'm not better than anyone else, I'm not more worthy of this ground I'm standing on—but I'm not less worthy, either. I'm allowed to be here, just as I am. Not only that—there are some damn good reasons to have me around.*

This isn't just about accepting yourself—this is about cele-brating who you were made to be. I don't have to be good at everything. I have other gifts.

This is the untangling of *what you're worth* from *what you're like*. Worth is separate. Your gifts don't make you worth more. Your faults don't make you worth less. A dinged-up old quarter and a shiny new one are both worth the same twenty-five cents. The coins don't have to prove their worth, and neither, I think, do we. They're worth those cents just because they exist, just because that's what it means to be a quarter.

I know what I am. I'm fully human, learning and growing and figuring things out. I am a work in progress, *and* I am a child of God, made in the image of love, made to be love on earth, even if I was not made to plan anybody's calendar.

Jessica flashed a smile at me and then got back to doing what she does best, which is creating a circle of human connection. I did not take the calendar, but I did take a deep breath—and then I practiced using my own gift for not making eye contact, so as to avoid accidentally volunteering for anything else. People are like that. We have flaws and gifts, and one does not cancel out the other. We are both/and. I don't know how it all works. It's a mystery, and I do not understand everything about all the mysteries. But that's okay. I have other gifts.

CHAPTER 20

Here I Am

Permission to Be Present

At this moment, I know where I am. I am in my office, a tiny little space that was once a closet in my bedroom. I am sitting on a meditation cushion that I have placed on the seat of my desk chair. My fingers are on the keyboard; my wrists are resting on the bamboo surface of my desk. I am cold, as usual, so I am wearing what my kids call my "sheep socks" and I have a zip-up sweatshirt on over my long-sleeved T-shirt and jeans. I am right here, right now, but most of the time it's surprisingly difficult to be where I am. Most of the time, I'm not even sure where I belong. Do I belong in my head, where my thoughts are fast and very noisy, or do I belong in the world, where you have to show up and feel things? Even when I try to hole up in my own head, people keep talking to me like I'm still in the room. Which I guess I am.

My daughter Evelyn does not have this problem. She is

where she is, always, whether that is at home or in the car or at the library or at the park. At church on Sundays, Evelyn is always very present. For a long while, she would use that time to empty out my purse like it was her job and she was trying to win Employee of the Month. (She was actually just a toddler, and we were not breaking any child labor laws.)

I would take out my sunglasses and my phone and the square of chocolate I had hidden in a zipped pocket, because those might not survive her love and attention. Then I would let her have at it.

Eli would watch over her shoulder and snatch up anything that might be useful for making noise.

Sunglasses case: yes. You can bang that on the folding chairs to keep the beat.

Keys: good for jingling, okay, yes.

For everything else he was the Put It Away Police, trying to stuff all the things back where they came from—which then gave Ev more to take out.

This is what we call "teamwork."

It is also what we call "keeping them happy while the grown-ups sing and stuff."

Because I would like to sing, in my warbling, off-key way. Matthew might be up front, choosing songs that invite us to be brave and to be love, songs reminding us that no one gets to tell us we don't belong. Or it might be Jessica up there, with a song assuring us that no one else knows what they're doing, either— not really. These are good reasons to make some noise, but it's hard to do that when little people are trying to take off out of the building. I had to assume they intended to play tag with the speeding traffic outside. Or maybe they were just trying to remember which direction led to the playground. Either way, life was easier if they stayed put and dumped all my personal belongings out under everyone's feet.

So that was our routine for a while, and it's what we were doing when the band started up with a song that went: *Here I am.* I'm pretty sure there were other words too, but I don't remember the other ones. I was stuck on the *here I am* part. Sometimes I'm not excited about songs with a lot of "I" in them, because even if I'm not technically the worst—even if I'm technically just human—I'm still nothing to sing home about, you know. I have good intentions, but I'm inconsistent and I miss things and I mess things up. This is not, as a general rule, what I want to focus my singing energy on.

But we sang, and Evelyn kept at her work.

Here I am, and out came my wallet and notebook. *Here I am,* and she pulled out a matchbox car and another notebook.

Here I am. She found three seashells that looked like tiny unicorn horns, because when someone says, "Mom, hold this," I hear, "Would you drop this into the bottomless fathoms of your purse and carry it around until neither one of us can remember where it came from? Thanks."

Here I am. A black pen. A green pen. A purple pen. A different kind of black pen. Forty-seven Band-Aids. Millions of tiny hair ties in rainbow colors. A turkey feather and another pen.

All the things I carry, spilled out over folding chairs and blue carpet. This is what I've got. This is what my days are made of. A turkey feather and a gross of pens.

You might think I would have more useful things in there, but no. That was everything. (Well, minus the previously relocated chocolate.)

I'm like the little hummingbirds that build nests in our back-yard. They gather twigs and sticks and bird fluff and mold it all into something recognizable in the crooks of the trees. The nest-building is very much a "let's see what we can do with what we have here" situation.

What did we have here?

I had hair ties to restore order in a very small way, for a very little while.

I had matchbox cars to meet someone right where they were, in their car seat and their boredom.

I had pens and journals to mark the moments, because my memory is like the colander I use to drain spaghetti: it holds the big stuff, but everything else washes away almost immediately.

I had my chocolate square because—come *on* now, chocolate doesn't need a "because." I feel like we've been over this already.

I don't know what the turkey feather was doing in there. Maybe somewhere a turkey was cold.

Here I am.

Not *here I try hard*, not *here I keep score*, not *here I am doing my best to be bigger and better*. Honestly, those would all make lousy songs. I don't want to meditate on any of those ideas. They're not the things I want to celebrate; they're just what I do when I'm not paying enough attention.

Here I am.

Those words were getting under my skin.

Here I am, I guess, but so what? What good does that do?

I've been trying to figure out what I have to offer the world if I'm not going to try to fix myself or let you know I'm the worst. I've got a few good qualities and some practice at living into wholeness at this point, but it doesn't feel like much to offer.

How is any of that helpful in a world suffering from poverty, conflict, hunger, homelessness, injustice, oppression, and waste (this is only a partial list)?

Here I am, and yes, I'm trying to be who I was made to be—but should I even be bothering about the crap in my head and heart when there are other things to do, things like serving and bridge-building and demanding justice for all? Does this stuff inside me even matter?

Does learning to show up as your whole self in the world really help? Does getting in touch with your true self make a difference? Does knowing that you are who you are for a damn good reason change anything?

Here I am, and I am just me. This hardly seems worth mentioning.

But then I remember that your self, your true self, cannot see itself as separate; not separate from everyone else, and not separate from love. And I remember that if you want to have the energy to make things better, you have to stop pretending not to need healing. Your own stuff will keep getting in the way until you deal with it. You can't see clearly while you're carrying your own pain all over the place.

That's why the stuff inside you matters. Because you need healing, and you are part of the whole, so healing yourself is part of healing the world. And as you do that—as you uncover more of who you are, as you learn that you are love and that in the great constellation of love, you are one of an infinite number of stars—you find you can't help but see the same about everyone else. You can't *not* want healing for everyone, freedom for everyone, air to breathe and room to grow for everyone. Your true self knows you are not separate from the world, so your healing is the world's healing, and the world's healing is yours. You can't help but get quiet and listen to people who have known this all along. You can't help but want to see everyone whole and healthy and free. And the more you know who you are, the more you see what you have to offer. You start where you are, and you do what you can.

That would be another way to understand *here I am*. Here I am, and I will work toward becoming more aware, so I don't push my own pain back out into the world. Here I am, present and paying attention—to what needs to be changed in the world, and to what needs to change within me, too. Here I am, remembering that these things—healing yourself, and participating in the healing of the world—are not opposed. You do not choose one instead of the other. You can work toward dismantling harmful systems in the world and dismantling lies in your heart at the same time. We need both, all, at once.

Here I am says: *I will not believe the lie that we are separate islands, that your pain doesn't affect me and my pain can't touch you.*

Here I am says: *I will see you, with your specific experience and history and identity. I will pay attention, and I will not ignore what I see.*

Here I am says: *I will be present to the pain and the confusion and the frustration AND the joy in this world. We will be present with and for each other. We will meet each other where we are.*

And what if this is our offering? *Here I am.*

It may not be much, but it's what I have. Waiting and hoping to come up with a more impressive gift later, when I've figured everything out and can follow all the rules and know just what to do, helps no one. Deciding that this—showing up as I am, doing what I can—will have to do, is simpler. It's where we start.

Here I am, child. Here I am, family. Here I am, world. Here I am, God. Here I am, with my forty-seven Band-Aids and my turkey feather. Band-Aids don't even fix anything. They just make space for the healing.

Here I am.

Here I am, with my history, my issues, and my ideas. Here I am, imperfect, a little worn out, with mismatched socks and unruly hair. Here I am.

Here is my perspective. Here is my personality. Here is my person. Here is my presence.

Maybe that's all we can do. Maybe that's the beginning of everything.

This is what I have left to offer the world if I'm not going to fix myself up first. I can't offer you perfection. I can't offer you an impressive, sparkly version of myself, one with a cape that will swoop in and solve all the problems. (That version of me would wear tall, shiny boots, for the record.)

All I have left is . . . *me*. The real me. My whole, true self, because when all of me shows up, I start to see what that self can do in the world—my real, whole self—because when we do show up, fully ourselves, fully human, that starts to change the story for everyone else, too. Showing up says, quietly, that I am not ashamed of my humanity, and that you don't need to be ashamed of yours, either. Showing up makes space for showing up. Living in wholeness makes space for more living in wholeness.

That's my offering, then. Be me. Be real. And make space for everyone else, too.

What else do I have, really? Does anybody want my hair ties?

Here you are: your own, only self. Here you are: the only one of you there ever was.

When you hold still long enough to notice, all the pieces add up to something. Even the hummingbird gets something useful in the end, the sticks and fluff all coming together into a little mud cup of a house. Her mixed-up pieces become exactly what she needs for this season. She knows better than to expect this moment to last forever. She has what she needs for here and now, and she rests in it.

There are gifts in the showing up. There's the gift of connection, because my whole self is here and open. There's the gift of gratitude, because how can I not be grateful once I see that this moment right here is enough? There's the gift of a grounded presence, not distracted by the past or the future, not hiding, not dodging, not pretending, just present. And there's the gift of making space for everyone else.

I am not wishing I was somewhere else. I am not expecting here to be different. Here I am.

I only have one chance to be in this moment. I only have one chance to be in every moment. Here I am.

When I bring all the parts of me out into the light—the pens and the Band-Aids and the chocolate and the turkey feather, too—when I pull the good stuff and the rest all together into my own, whole self: *Here I am.*

Forever is composed of nows, says the Emily Dickinson poem, and I want to be part of that forever, purse spilled out over the floor and all. Here I am.[1]

Maybe *here I am* is the best and most beautiful thing we have to offer.

Here is Evelyn, all curiosity.

Here is Eli, making a joyful noise.

Here am I, full of questions.

Here you are, all of you.

Here I am. This is the point of being here. This is everything I have to offer: here I am.

CHAPTER 21

Grace in the Mess

Permission to Offer More

A toddler—any toddler—who is out of your sight for 8.4 seconds will find their way into your phone, open up the Amazon app, and accidentally order a new bike and a wheel of cheese. That is just how toddlers work.

It used to be that when parents looked away to sneeze or something, toddlers would climb the kitchen counters and eat all the cookies that were hidden up there. Now, instead, we're all one unsupervised click away from being the proud owners of size 11 bowling shoes or a book on how to identify wild carrots.

I'm not sure it's an improvement, honestly. It's not what I was hoping for in the evolution of toddlerhood.

There is probably a list for this somewhere on the internet: *6 DIY Projects to Make with the Immersion Blender and the Toe Socks Your Toddler Ordered When You Weren't Looking!* Number three is a succulent planter.

The internet has a list for everything. Top 3 Tantrum-Busting Guitar Solos. The 7 Foods to Stop Eating before Your Hair Falls Out. Five Best Tips for Organizing the Disaster That Is Your Kitchen and Let's Not Even Talk about Your Closets. I even found one called 10 Ways to Calm Everyday Anxieties.

This is, obviously, an area of interest.

"Do something with your hands," the article said. "Try knitting," it said, "or worry beads."

What are worry beads, I wondered?

Are they easier than learning to knit? I looked it up. Oh, worry beads are the same as prayer beads. Aha.

I put that information on the shelf of "things I will probably never think about again, even though they may be helpful or interesting," right next to the DIY immersion blender/succulent planter, and there it sat, very quiet and tidy.

It stayed on that shelf in my brain right up until I noticed an email from Amazon the next morning. *Good news! The prayer beads you bought with one-click ordering have now shipped!*

The what are what, now?

Okay.

So.

When you are worried that your kids are going to do something embarrassing or inappropriate or accidental, like place surprise orders over the internet, that is how you know you are about to do that thing yourself. My kids had accidentally ordered nothing. *I* had accidentally ordered prayer beads.

I logged on to my account, but there was no option for "stop delivery on thing I did not mean to order."

When you fill out the return form, under "reason for return" there is no box to check for "I guess I touched the 'buy with one click' button on my phone screen when I, out of sheer curiosity, price-checked this item."

I marked the box for "I changed my mind" instead.

Self, I thought, *you are fired from looking at things on the internet.*

Self, I thought, *you are kind of a mess. The kind of mess that purchases perfumed strings of sandalwood beads without even knowing it.*

See, I forgot what I believed for a minute there. I forgot who I was.

I don't mean that I forgot to be the kind of person who doesn't accidentally order prayer beads over the internet. That isn't happening. I will probably always be the kind of person who does things like accidentally ordering prayer beads over the internet.

That's the same kind of person who forgets to put the most important ingredient on the grocery list every single time. I'm still that person, too. But I knew that, I did.

No, I forgot to practice seeing the truth about myself and saying, *It's okay. You don't have to be perfect.* I forgot to be the kind of person who says, *It's cool. Everything belongs. Doing ridiculous things does not mean you're broken. This is part of the story, too. No big deal.*

But then I remembered. I remembered all the things I've been learning about living in wholeness and truth and grace.

Grace, you know, is what happens when love shows up in time and space. Grace is what love does in the world, in your life, in your soul. It's love arriving, reminding you of who you are, and turning you back toward the truth of your belonging, right here, as you are. When you remember who you are, you can show up. You can be your whole self. Grace and truth and living in wholeness—they work together. That's what I've been learning.

And I've been learning that truth and grace make pretty much everything better.

There was an evening when one of my kids was having a hard time getting into bed. It had been a hard few nights in a row, honestly, and the thing I want to do when a person is awake long past bedtime is to say I LOVE YOU, AND RIGHT NOW I WOULD LOVE FOR YOU TO BE IN YOUR BED, YES YOU MAY LIE THERE AWAKE UNTIL MORNING JUST PLEASE STAY PUT OKAY THANKS.

But instead I tried really, really hard to remember what it feels like to be the person whose body is being a little bit unco-operative and irritated and irrational. (It turned out not to be a stretch. I am familiar with that feeling. I have that feeling twice a week, at least. That is what my own personal brand of mess is made of: giant feelings and a general inability to play along with the ways of the world.)

So I climbed into a top bunk and lay down next to my fully awake youngling.

I figured feeling not-alone might help.

"You know," I said, "what happens to me, when I am lying in bed and cannot fall asleep is, sometimes I start to feel scared. Sometimes I start to feel worried. I feel scared about all kinds of things that do not feel scary during the day, and I feel worried about all kinds of things that will probably never happen. I just feel afraid."

"YES," my kiddo said. "YES, that is it exactly. Me too."

So I told her about how gratitude and fear cannot live in our bodies at the same time. They're opposites. One fills up all the space, and the other can't find anywhere to hold on, so you only get to have one at a time. You have to choose.

I told her about making a list of as many thankful things as you can think of while you lie there in the dark, awake and alone. (I told her how she's never really alone.)

"Let's make *you* a list," I said. "I'll help. I think your list would start like this:

"*First*, I am thankful for my mom, who is charming and funny and also awesome and cool.

"Next, I am thankful again for my mom, who makes amazing snacks and is also awesome and fun.

"And I am thankful for my mom, who always gets me the best library books and is pretty much just all-around awesome.

"Then I am also thankful for my dad, who is basically as cool as my mom."

("I feel like this list would be different if Dad were making it," she said, but she was laughing by then, which I took as a good sign.)

Together we thought of other things to put on the list, and after a few minutes, I climbed down the bunk bed ladder, squeezed both of her hands, and told her I would come back to check on her in a while to see how it was going.

She was asleep before I came back, and I put that on my own list of thankful things.

I worry, sometimes, that I have given my kids all of my most difficult quirks, like insomnia and middle-of-the-night fears, an inability to avoid accidental Amazon orders, big feelings and doubts and the self-confidence of a gnat. (Maybe not that last one.) I feel terrible about this. How did I not help them avoid all of my hard things? How? Wasn't that my job, to give them the best things and to keep everything else—insecurities, anxieties, discomfort, the toilet cleaner—out of reach?

Maybe, or maybe not, but there is also this: I am the way I am for a damn good reason, and I don't have to be ashamed of all my mistakes and my feeling of not fitting in the world and my inability to follow rules someone else invented. If my kids ended up with some of those same hard things, well, I've been down those roads before, and I know a thing or two about how to face the boulders in the path. And if I'll go to those hard places with her, if I'll walk alongside her, my beloved child gets to know she is seen, she is not alone, and she is absolutely allowed to be the person she is. Everything belongs, even the hard things.

I still forget that sometimes, and I divide myself up into good parts and unacceptable parts, with light and cheery parts on one side and embarrassing and painful parts on the other. I decide some of me is allowed and some should stay hidden—some is worthy of passing on, and some of me ought to be stamped out. As though that were up to me to decide. And when the shadow parts do not disappear, I start building that shiny outside shell again so that no one will notice.

But because of grace, I remember: this is who I was made to be. I am who I am—exactly as I am, and exactly as I will become—for a damn good reason. We all are.

Grace points us straight back to the truth. The truth is, you—the person you are, the person you were made to be—are a loved child of God. You are good, and you are loved. You are, in fact, connected to all the love in the universe. You are not separate. You are part of the whole, imperfect, wildly spinning thing. You are seen and known and loved, exactly as you are. And when you know who you are, you act like it.

When I remember about grace, I can move again. I can breathe. I am braver, because I know that even if I accidentally order strings of sandalwood beads over the internet, even if I do something worse than that (which, let's face it, *I will*), I won't be—I can't be—loved any less. And the truth of who I am calls out to the truth of who you are. The truth of who I am says, *You're kind of a mess? Me too.* Me too, but so what? The mess doesn't define us. It might be *where* we are, but it isn't *who* we are. None of us, not a single one of us, will ever quit making stupid mistakes and falling apart and getting lost and trying to hide ourselves again from time to time. All of us will keep doing *something.* I'm never going to love myself into flawlessness, and I can't accept myself into perfection. There will always be some messiness, but reaching for grace is simpler than hiding in shame.

That's the truth. Even if I sometimes forget.

The truth is simple, but believing it is not easy. Easy, for me, is to name the mess that is me, and to decide it means I don't belong here, wherever here is. That is so easy, I can do it without thinking. Simplicity is harder. Simplicity looks like accepting that I am human, and that being human involves getting things wrong, but also that it's okay to be human. Simplicity, in other words, looks like truth and grace.

The truth is, we are, all of us, human. We're all falling apart in one way or another. Sometimes we forget who we are, and who we are meant to be. Sometimes we forget to treat each other and ourselves and our world with kindness. We don't score high marks in the patience and gentleness categories some days.

The truth is, we all need grace. We all need love to arrive, to remind us of who we are, and to turn us back to the truth of our belonging, again and again and again.

We all need the truth: that we don't have to have all the answers. That we don't have to get everything right. That we don't have to fix ourselves. That we are loved in our imperfection and our mess, and that our imperfection and mess do not stop us from being love. That grace meets you—your real, whole self—right where you are, now, today.

Grace does not take away the messiness of being human, but it does, at least, change how I respond when I realize there are surprise prayer beads speeding their way to me from South Carolina.

I can offer myself patience.

I can show myself kindness.

I can forgive the guy who invented one-click shopping, that I cannot now figure out how to turn off.

I can remember that my purpose is to be love. My purpose isn't "make no mistakes."

I can shake my head and laugh at myself.

I can be human. That's kind of what I'm here to do.

I'm here to keep showing up, to keep wading through the weeds of the everyday.

I'm here to keep on being my whole self, even though I remember who I am, and I forget who I am, sometimes both in the same breath.

And I'm here to tell the truth.

The truth is that even though being human means being kind of a mess, grace meets me in the mess if I let it. I won't outgrow it, and I won't stop needing it—but it hasn't outgrown me, either, and it's just waiting for me. That's how things get better. Not by fixing, but by being who we are, owning the truth of who we are, and inviting more of ourselves out into the light of grace, every day.

CHAPTER 22

Forget the Map

Permission to Be Who You Were Made to Be

Evelyn and I have a routine for when I'm heading out the door to go anywhere at all. It goes like this: I get my jacket and purse, I double-check that I have my phone and my wallet, I try to pull on my shoes, and she wraps her little arms around my body in an attempt to either slow me down or get me to take her along. This works for neither of us, really, but even if Ev doesn't get what she wants on this one, she does at least get to express her desires through words and body language, and I guess that is a good skill to practice.

The last time I went to Bonnie's house, Evelyn wove her arms around my legs so that by the time I'd found my car keys in my bag, I couldn't move. "I want to go," she said.

I tried to get down to her eye level, but vertical motion was not among my options unless I wanted to squish her. Squishing is not my preferred method of escape. "I know, but I'm just going to Bonnie's," I told her. Bonnie's house is ten minutes away. I was not embarking on a journey; I was driving over the hill and past the grocery store. "I'll come kiss you in your bed when I get home."

"I want to go to Bonnie's," she said. "I *looooooooove* Bonnie." This is true; once, Bonnie and her husband, Dave, drove us home from church, and Evelyn has loved them ever since. Bonnie thinks this is because Dave gave the kids tortilla chips in the car, but it might also be because Evelyn loves pretty much everyone. Ev will walk into a room full of strangers and say, "Look at all the friends we haven't met!" She did not get this from me, obviously.

"You do love Bonnie!" I agreed. "You do. But you know what? There are no toys at Bonnie's house. The only things at Bonnie's house are us boring grown-ups. You wouldn't have anything fun to do."

I could see the hope in her eyes then, because she had an answer for this. She can think of an answer to nearly anything, a skill she learned from every one of her siblings before her. "I'll just sit and watch you! I'll just sit there. At Bonnie's. Pleeeeeease?" She squeezed my legs to her chest, pressing her cheek against me in something like a hug. "I will just be with you."

I did not know the best way to extricate myself from those arms and that conversation. She wasn't worried about being away from me; she just held firm to her position that going out was always more delightful than staying home. (Again, not a thing she learned from me.) She would be happy again after I walked out the door, I knew. It was only the leaving that was hard.

It's true that between Abigail and Owen and Audrey and Sadie and Eli and Ev, I have had over a decade to practice this maneuver, and I still don't have it down. I have learned a couple of things, though. I have learned how to tell when a little person will be okay without me, and when something deeper is going on. I have learned which distractions have a chance of working, and which ones are a waste of my breath. But how to rationalize with a pre-rational preschooler? That, I continue to have no idea about. Not one clue.

I also didn't know, at that moment, if the sweatshirt I was wearing would be warm enough for the night, whether my phone would fall through the little rip in my jeans pocket as I walked to the car, if I would get to Bonnie's house fifteen minutes early or (more likely) thirty minutes late, or if we had ingredients in the pantry for the next morning's breakfast.

And that's just the small stuff. I still didn't understand how other people always knew what to say or do in any given situation, or why I could never write a simple email without considering my words from eight different angles, or why I second-guessed every choice and rehashed every awkward thing I ever said forever, or why all of this seemed so much easier for everyone else.

I thought I would know more of these things by now, is all. I thought I would have some of them figured out.

I used to have an idea of how life should be—how *I* should be—and honestly, it looked good. It looked like a place where I would never be stressed, never be running late, never be anxious about what to wear or whether I had time to dry my hair. I would never forget things, like my purse or my phone or my neighbor's first name. I would be confident, with shiny hair and keys that I could locate at any time. I expected to arrive there by the time I was a real grown-up. That's how I would know I was a fully qualified human, see? I would be living in the Land of Ease. That's how I would know. The Land of Ease is a place where I would be myself, but that self would be *better* than this one, so everything would be easier. That was the idea.

It is possible that the map in my head—the map from here to there, the one showing my ultimate destination, even if the path was a little fuzzy—was cobbled together out of glossy magazines, big-screen movies, and chipper Facebook status updates. I'm not sure. But I used to believe that, eventually, I would get there, to the place where I would always be freshly scrubbed and respectable, where I would always have it all together, where I would have arrived. I didn't ever have an exact plan for how to get there, though, because the map was less clear about that. Copying the other people, following the good old GRC, taking care of all the *shoulds*—these were my guesses, but they never got me very far. Maybe the answer was magic? Magic combined with time and practice, I guess. I used to expect that this glittering place was just what life was supposed to look like. (My actual life looks more like being roommates with a very small tornado.)

All I could see, looking at that map, was where I *wasn't*. When all you can see is what isn't working, you can't really tell who you are and who you're meant to be. You can't see that you were made in the image of God if the image you project onto yourself is broken.

And if this is true—if you were made in the image of the divine—what does that make you?

In this case, it made me late getting to Bonnie's house.

By the time we convinced Evelyn that going out with me would not be nearly as marvelous as reading a Very Long Book about Mercy Watson, Pig Extraordinaire, with Dane, I was running behind. When I finally made it to Bonnie's, the rest of our little group of love warriors was already gathered around the kitchen island choosing snacks. (Talking and listening is hard work. Sustenance is required.) We chatted in groups of two or three while we loaded up our plates and poured our drinks. I was carrying my mug of ginger-turmeric tea to the couch when I overheard something Jessica said. Jessica was the one who first taught me that we are the way we are for a good reason, so I tend to listen when she talks (even when she's not talking to me, apparently). I heard her say, "Oh, I'm learning about *that* from my friend Melissa."

"You're learning something from *me*? What are you learning from me?"

I was afraid it might be something like *I'm learning how to be the worst by watching Melissa*, but Jessica isn't really the evil sarcastic type, and anyway, she reached behind her to where I was standing and squeezed my hand after she said it. You don't squeeze someone's hand right after saying how awful they are.

No, she explained, she and I had been talking lately about how our surroundings affect us, how we feel differently in different spaces. Jess had moved to a new house, and she was thinking about how she wanted to settle in. She had been learning about this—about intentionally creating spaces that felt how she wanted them to feel—from me.

The cranky voice in my head started to pipe up to tell me what it thought about that, but all it could come up with was, "What? Wait, what?" It was like finding an unexpected clue in a mystery—you know it's important, but you can't quite figure out how it all fits together at first. *She's learning from me. She's learning from ME? But I'm not the best. I'm not perfect, and she's learning stuff from me. Does she know I don't have it all together?* (She does.) *Doesn't she know that disqualifies me from—well, everything?*

But she is learning from me.

I guess she can do that because she's been practicing something *else*. Jess practices believing that humans do not get sorted into two groups, one for humans who have it all together (from whom you take advice), and one for humans who are a mess (to whom you try not to get too close). She knows that we're all both/and. We're all flailing *and* we're all worth listening to.

I had not spent most of my days practicing that. I believed for so long that I could either be perfect or I could be the worst, and if I wasn't measuring up, I somehow didn't count. I used to think that the either/or way—the way of believing in my own brokenness, the way of hiding, the way of scolding myself and keeping score so that I always came out the loser—would get me closer to being all good all the time, but instead, it convinced me I was the worst. I always knew that humans were never meant to be either/or kinds of creatures, but I forgot that meant me, too. I'm both/and. We're all both/and. That's why I don't have to figure everything out before I can be okay; I can be loved and a mess all at once. Being a person is about learning to show up, even with my faults and flaws and needs and neuroses showing. None of them define me.

Which brings me back to the question of what *does* define me. If I am a child of God, what does that make me?

I don't know all the things about God, because I'm human, and because I'm learning to be okay with mystery. I do know that whatever else God is, underneath it all, God is love. Love is not what God *does*, love is who God *is*, and love is who I was made to be, too. I was made to be love on earth—love walking around with a body and a history and a giant stack of dirty dishes waiting for my attention in the kitchen. Whatever else I am, underneath it all, I am love.

And, again, I'm pretty sure it's okay to be human, since I can't be anything else. If it is—if it's okay to be human, and humans don't always get things right—then it's *also* okay to stop practicing all the things that are supposed to make me "better." I don't have to be better than human. I actually can't.

That place I was always trying to get to, the one where my purse would not be overflowing with pens and tissues, the one where I would arrive everywhere on time, the one where I would never be embarrassed or ashamed or lonely—that isn't a place where humans live. That isn't a place where we can struggle and grow and overcome. That's not where relationships are forged by walking together through tragedy and heartache and through rising and enduring and through grieving and even, sometimes, through wild, unrestrained joy. That place—that perfect, imaginary place—isn't where life happens. The map is a lie. The destination is a mirage, and the path never gets there.

Life happens in the real world, the one with tangled hair and dust bunnies and missing charger cords—and hot tea and laughter and sunshine and hope. That's the world that was made for humanity. We aren't supposed to escape it; we're supposed to live in it.

So okay, fine. I'm not trying to get to a better, easier reality anymore. I am practicing being here, where Jess reminds me I am both/and. I'm here, where the goal is to know who you are, to show up in your life and in your days, to pay attention, to be who you were made to be. To be love. That's what I'm trying to do now.

This is an entirely different path. This one wasn't marked on the old map at all, maybe because it's not very flashy. There's dirt under my nails on this path, and mud on my shoes. There are rocks and fallen branches in the road, and it's not easy, but it is real. This is where I am now.

Getting comfortable with who you are (beloved and dear, messy and full of contradiction, with misperceptions and limits) and who you were made to be (love) is simpler than following any map that claims it will make you better.

I am where I am. I am who I am. I am what I am.

And what I am—what is in me—is the good stuff *and* the embarrassing stuff. It's both. It's all.

Who needs me to be perfect, anyway? Not Jessica, apparently. Not any of our friends. Not Dane. He's never asked me to inch closer to flawlessness. I don't even think he knows what that is supposed to look like. (He's not on Instagram much.) Not my kids. They want a real parent, not a perfect one. No one asks why I forget things or lose things or try things that don't work. They do not say, "Our lives would be better if you were a little less weird," or "Could you just stay in your room where you won't get in our way?"

They don't seem to expect me to be especially impressive.

There haven't been any thunderbolts from heaven, either, or ominous ravens on my balcony, tilting their heads and following me with their yellow eyes. It's as though God isn't even trying to send me signs about how disappointing I am.

It's just me. I'm the only one who wanted me to be perfect. It would be the very best shame escape, because what is there to be ashamed of if you're perfect? You would never accidentally hurt anyone, or say something inappropriate, or find out you were wrong about everything. That would be simplest, if it were possible. But it isn't. In a world where perfect doesn't exist, the next simplest option is to *believe the truth*. The truth is that being a person is complicated. The truth is, you aren't going to get everything right. The truth is, you can be who you are in the world—because you are who you are for a damn good reason, and underneath it all, you are love, and you are loved.

It was only me who thought I had to be a little bit better before I could be okay. It was only me who thought I was broken. It was only me.

But I already have everything I need to live in wholeness. I already know who I am. I am real, and I am messy, and I am awkward, and I am figuring things out, and I am *still* love.

When you know that—when you know that you are not broken, that you are human—you know that everyone else is, too. You are not separate, not from each other and certainly not from love. You are not separate. You are not alone.

You were made to be the person you are, and the person you are—the self you are underneath everything else, your true self—is good. That is the truth about you. That is the truth about me. The truth does not include being perfect. I was following a map that was supposed to get me there, but perfect isn't even a place I can go. The search for perfect is a road with no destination, and I want to get somewhere. I want to get to the place where I can hear the voice of love without a bunch of other noise getting in the way. The road to get *there* looks like showing up, being your real self, and making space for all the other travelers along the way.

Instead of asking, *Am I worse than everyone else? Am I getting this wrong?* The new questions are, *Am I showing up? Am I being myself? Am I listening to the voice of love, or have I gotten tripped up again, running from fear or hiding from shame?*

When you're listening to the voices of fear and shame—the

voices that know all about expectations and how you're not meeting them—you can't hear the truth about who you are. You can't hear the truth that you are loved just as you are—right here and right now. You just can't. But when you move closer to the voice of love, you move closer to truth and beauty and fierce goodness. You move closer to all the things with which love keeps company: grace and peace and grounded presence, kindness and bravery and true selflessness.

This is the new map, then. This is the new plan: Keep coming back to the truth. The truth is love. The path looks like following the love.

If my old mantra sounded like, *I am the worst,* my new one sounds like, *Here I am, all of me. This is who I was made to be.* I don't have to become anything else, because my true self, the self underneath all the labels and masks and ways of being I've collected, has always been enough. The me behind the shield, the me who is a beloved child of God, full stop—that truest, underneath-it-all, at-my-core self—is already everything it needs to be. Accepted. Loved. Love.

What I get to do now, what I get to do forever, is practice stripping away everything I've ever brought in to cover up that self, everything I've ever hidden behind: every "yes" that should have been a no, every "I'm fine" that should have been an "I'm drowning," every busy afternoon that should have been a refuge, every moment of quiet that should have been a rebellion. I get to practice letting go of everything that makes me feel shielded and safe and contained. I'm not here to change who I am; I'm here to be who I was made to be. The work is in showing up and reaching out from the truest place I can.

The only way to do that is to listen for the voice of love. I'm practicing sifting it out from the voice of shame. The voice of shame never tells the whole story.

The whole story starts when you show up as your whole self.

I still make every conversation awkward. I'm still worried coyotes might be stalking my backyard. I still forget that everything belongs, and that grace means I am welcome, right here and right now. I still have to remind myself to tell the truth when someone asks how I am. *I'm still me.* I'm still not perfect.

You know why? Because I'm human, and human is a perfectly good thing to be.

Back at Bonnie's house, sitting on the big couch next to Jessica, I decided to believe that. I would sit with these women who did not expect me to be perfect, and then I would go home to Dane, who does not expect me to be perfect, and to my children, who just want me to be present. I will be who I am, with them and for them—and for me, too.

You are the way you are for a damn good reason. I don't know all your reasons. I don't know why you are *all* the ways you are. But I do know that one of the reasons you are you is just because you're human. Being human means you aren't going to get it right all the time. You won't always know the best things to do or the right things to say. You're going to make mistakes. That's okay. When you know who you are apart from all of that, when you know what love says about you—it's all okay.

Love says, *Go ahead, get back up, try again.*

Love says, *I'm not keeping score.*

Love says, *It is good. You are loved.*

Love says, *You're human, and you were made to be human on purpose.*

Underneath the good and the not-so-good, underneath

everything else, humans were made to be one thing. You are the way you are for a lot of good reasons, but you are *human* for one reason. So am I. So are all of us. You know what the reason is.

The reason is simple.

The reason is love.

CHAPTER 23

These Are the Questions

Permission to Be Free

My son, Owen, would like us all to know that word problems are terrible. He was fourteen when he voiced this opinion, so I thought he was talking about *solving* word problems or something, but that is not what he meant.

"Think about this," he said. "'Your friend has 127 pineapples. If he gives you 46 and you eat 23, how many pineapples do you each have left?' *That* is not the biggest question I have about this situation."

Okay, so he had a point.

I felt like the real question would be, "Which one of you will vomit first?"

My sister, Ryleigh, suggested, "What will you do when your friend falls into a funky pineapple-sugar coma?"

Maybe the best question was really, "How will you practice your healthy intervention skills here? Will you go straight to,

'John, it's time to lay off the tropical fruit' or will you start with, 'There are a lot of interesting diets in the world, buddy, but all-pineapple isn't the one for you'?"

But no, Owen's word problem just wanted to know about pineapple math.

It's easy to focus on the wrong thing, is what I'm saying here. We all do it, all the time.

We ask what's wrong with us instead of asking what needs to change in the world. We ask how to hide our shame instead of listening for the voice of love. We wonder why everyone else has it all together when we're still awkward and squirming. *We're focusing on the wrong questions.*

Here is what I want to tell you. You can go through life being who you think you're supposed to be. You can. You can pretend to really be the person everyone else thinks you should be. You can figure out enough of the rules to play the game. You can try hard to be close to perfect, and then you can try harder again, because you never actually get there. You can pretend and perform until the sun sets. You absolutely could do that. It's a lot of work and a lot of things to remember. But you could do it.

Or you can give yourself permission to be who you really are.

It's that simple. You can try to be someone else, which will keep you pushing and striving and redirecting because it never quite works, or you can stop. *You can stop.* You can listen for who you are and what you need. The important question is not, "What will they think?" or, "Am I allowed?" It's, "Who does the voice of love say I am, and how am I going to be that person, right here, right now?"

This is the simpler path, and it really is better.

It means settling into your skin, and into your life, and into yourself. It means being okay with not being liked by everyone or even understood all the time. It's looking at yourself, as you are, and saying, "It's all okay." My friend Jessilyn told me to try this, and she is the kind of person who has a real morning routine with quiet and meditation every day. She knows how to practice listening. She told me to try saying to myself, *That thing you're embarrassed about? That thing you got wrong? That thing you wish wasn't true about you? Yeah, it's true. But it's okay.*

It's saying to yourself, *I see you, and you are loved.* It's knowing you're secure.

This simpler way looks like being able to hold still. It's being able to look in the mirror *and* being able to close your eyes and look inside. It's being friends with the person you see.

It looks like belonging to yourself, and then being able to reach out to the people around you.

You can't find that when you're hiding and comparing and pretending to have it all together, in the arrive-on-time-with-shiny-hair sense. You can't find it when you're trying to meet expectations and aiming for perfect. You can't see it when you believe in your own brokenness.

But when you give yourself permission to let go of perfect and start settling into real—it's better. It's simpler. There's rest here.

It doesn't look like flipping a switch and becoming suddenly self-aware and present all the time, though. You don't become consistently self-improved just because you've decided to show up. Or at least I haven't. I'm inconsistent and forgetful, and I don't always get it right. But I know what to come back to now, when I lose my way. I know which direction I mean to walk. I don't have to look to anyone else to find that.

I want to tell you that knowing and being yourself—it isn't selfish. It isn't about paying attention to yourself instead of paying attention to everyone else. It's about knowing who you are so you can be that person in the world. It's about believing that you were made to be exactly who you are and how you are on purpose.

Because the truth is, you can try to be of service in the world without knowing who you are, but if you do that, you will be a placeholder, not a real presence, and you will burn out. Your real gift to the world begins when you show up as yourself.

Showing up is your testament to the fact that this world is a place of creativity and possibility and beauty. It's you staking your belief in truth and love—in the truth that you are loved, and the truth that you are love. You're made of love. The whole thing is built on love.

And that love invites you to tell a truer story about yourself and your place in the world. That story I used to believe, the one that said I was the worst—that one was wrong. It didn't have the truth of who I am in it, and the truth really will set you free.

My truer story sounds like this: *It is good to be who you were made to be, imperfect, awkward, and human. It is good to be your real, whole self, the self that is love.* That's it.

When you know who you are, when you know that you are loved, when you know that it is absolutely okay—that it is *good*—to be the person you were made to be, you're free. You're free from expectations, free from other people's good ideas about your life, free from pretending, free from hiding, free from wearing yourself thin on the treadmill of never-enough. Free from all the masks you've been wearing. Free from all the layers you've built up between you and the outside world. Free.

That's what we're doing here. That's what this whole book has been about. Free is step one. Step two is up to you.

Acknowledgments

Secretly, I love acknowledgments in books. It's like the last little bit of hot fudge after you've eaten your sundae—*Oh, you thought you were done? Not quite! There's a tiny bit more, if you want it!* Though some acknowledgments read more like dry toast crumbs when they *could* be chocolate sauce, and that's just sad. We'll see what we can do here.

Thanks goes first of all to *you*, you who read these words, who looked into these pages and saw yourself reflected back. I'm so glad you joined me here. Come hang out with me on the internet, we'll talk about all the things.

Thank you to Angela Scheff, who has the remarkable ability to invite me into both confidence and calm in the space of a single phone call. (I think we all understand what a feat this is.)

Thank you to Stephanie Smith, who is a champion of creativity and a tireless advocate for readers, and whose insight helped these words become what they are.

A million thanks to Alicia Kasen, Harmony Harkema, Robin Barnett, and the entire hardworking team at Zondervan, for bringing this book into being.

Thank you to Deborah at Tessera Editorial for helping me to open up the invitation in these pages.

Thank you, thank you, thank you to the friends who appear on these pages—Kate Christensen-Martin, Abi Cotler, Carrie Geremia, Colby Martin, Jessilyn Million, Sheena Nageli, Sarah Polzin, Bonnie Reveley, Dave Reveley, Matthew Blake Williams, and Jessica Winet—for pointing me toward light and love again and again and again.

To Bonnie and our entire band of love warriors, in all its various incarnations: I love you so. Janelle, thanks for manifesting us into being—that was super convenient.

Thank you to Jessica Mitchell for creating space, for seeing into the heart of things, for asking questions and holding out for answers, every time.

To Megan Pincus Kajitani, who read these words in the middle of everything, and who knew the answer when I asked whether I could really, truly do this: thank you.

Thank you to Liz Dennery, who first said the words "permission granted" to me, and was exactly right.

Thank you to Robyjean Bishop, who made so many things possible with her presence.

Thank you to Ry Beloin for all the late-night conversations—conversations less about these words, and more about the living of them. We will be sleepy forever, I think.

I could fill an entire other book thanking my personal heroes, the ones I've never met but whose lives and work have shaped the person I am. But given that you just finished reading this book, we can save that for another day. For now, thank you to those whose words shaped my own story as told between these covers: Maya Angelou, Brené Brown, Kelly Corrigan, Glennon Doyle, Rachel Held Evans, Elizabeth Gilbert, Anne Lamott, Richard Rohr, and Oprah Winfrey.

Abigail, Owen, Audrey, Sadie, Eli, and Evelyn, I can't believe how lucky I am that I get to be your mom, every day, forever. The wildest joy of my life is to know you, and to hang out with you, and to text you incessantly if you ever decide to do a ridiculous thing like go off to college or live on your own. (And I will. Just ask Abigail.) You are all the best.

And to Dane: well, now you know about the weird arm hair, so I guess that's everything. Thank you for trusting me, thank you for pushing me to start and then to keep going, thank you for giving me the words (just two of them, really) to talk back when it would be easier to stay quiet. I'm so glad this is our adventure.

Notes

CHAPTER 4: ABOUT THAT FIRE

1. Richard Rohr, *Immortal Diamond* (San Francisco: Jossey-Bass, 2013), xiii.
2. Ibid., 20.
3. Elizabeth Gilbert, "NOT THIS: Back by Popular Demand," https://www.facebook.com/GilbertLiz/posts/not-this-back-by -popular-demandsweet-friends-for-some-mysterious-reason -that-i-s/1004594839622631/, Facebook, April 12, 2016.
4. Brené Brown, *Braving the Wilderness* (New York: Random House, 2017), 115.

CHAPTER 10: THE DISTRACTION IS IN THE DETAILS

1. Richard Rohr, "Embracing the Shadow: God Sees in Wholes, We See in Parts," Center for Action and Contemplation (July 10, 2016), https://cac.org/god-sees-wholes-see-parts-2016–07–10/.
2. Richard Rohr, "Embracing the Shadow: Seeing Truly," Center for Action and Contemplation (July 15, 2016), https://cac.org/ seeing-truly-2016–07–15/.

CHAPTER 13: THIS ISN'T ABOUT YOU

1. Brené Brown, *The Gifts of Imperfection* (Center City, MN: Hazelden Publishing, 2010), 53–54.
2. Kelly Corrigan, *Tell Me More* (New York: Random House, 2018), vii.
3. Ibid., 27–50.

CHAPTER 15: KATE AT THE COFFEE SHOP

1. Kate introduced us to *eshet chayil* as written about in Rachel Held Evans's *A Year of Biblical Womanhood* (Nashville: Thomas Nelson, 2012), 74–98.

2. In Jewish families, *eshet chayil* is sung over the woman of the house as part of the blessing of Shabbat. In this instance, the phrase brought us joy and wisdom—and at the same time, the liturgy itself was appropriated from a culture and religion that was not our own.

CHAPTER 16: TRY SAYING THE TRUE THINGS

1. Glennon Doyle, *Love Warrior* (New York: Flatiron Books, 2016), 223.

CHAPTER 19: I HAVE OTHER GIFTS

1. Oprah Winfrey, Video: "The Powerful Lesson Maya Angelou Taught Oprah" (October 19, 2011), http://www.oprah.com/oprahs-lifeclass/the-powerful-lesson-maya-angelou-taught-oprah-video.

CHAPTER 20: HERE I AM

1. Ralph W. Franklin, ed., *The Poems of Emily Dickinson: Reading Edition* (Cambridge, MA: The Belknap Press of Harvard University Press, 1998), 690.